The Moses Hudgin Log House

THE MOSES HUDGIN LOG HOUSE

Six Generations On Prince Edward County's South Shore

by Laura Hudgin Edge

ONTARIO HISTORY PRESS

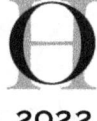

2022

© Copyright 2022 Laura Hudgin Edge

All rights reserved. No part of this publication may be reproduced, stored in a retrieval system, or transmitted, in any form or by any means, electronic, mechanical, photocopying, recording, or otherwise, without the prior written permission of the author.
The dynamic nature of the Internet can cause web addresses or links contained in this book to change, and they may no longer be valid after publication.
The views expressed in this work are solely those of the author and do not necessarily reflect the views of the publisher, and the publisher hereby disclaims any responsibility for them.

ISBN: 978-0-9940106-8-1

Title: The Moses Hudgin Log House: Six Generations
                  On Prince Edward County's South Shore

Author: Laura Hudgin Edge

Additional research by Marc Seguin

Publisher: Ontario History Press,
              Prince Edward County, Ontario, Canada. 2022

Editor: Marc Seguin

Comments and inquiries can be sent by email to the author at
press@ontariohistory.ca

This book is available at local bookstores, from major online book retailers, and at www.ontariohistory.ca

Front cover image: The Moses Hudgin Log House, by Bonita (Hudgin) Allen.
Back cover photograph: The Log House, June 2022, by Marc Seguin.
Cover design: Marc Seguin.

Table of Contents

Preface i

Acknowledgements iv

Introduction 1

Family Tree 5

Chapter 1 – The Log House 7

Chapter 2 – Family Origins 17

Chapter 3 – Life on the South Shore 27

Chapter 4 – The Next Generation 39

Chapter 5 – Into the 20th Century 55

Chapter 6 – The Last Generations 73

Chapter 7 – Restoring the Moses Hudgin Log House ... 81

Appendices 87

Sources Cited 97

Index 101

Preface

    My carefree summers as a child in Prince Edward County, Ontario, included the sun and sand at the Outlet beach, now part of the well-known Sandbanks Provincial Park. I loved building dribble sandcastles and fishing in the Outlet River.

    However, what made more of an impression on me was when my dad, Glen Hudgin, would take a detour down Ostrander Point Road on our way to our "secret beach" to make a stop at the Moses Hudgin log house. I recall the bumpy dirt road with many potholes often filled with rainwater. My sisters and I would squeal in delight at seeing the little green frogs jump from puddle to puddle to get out of the way. The family car would slow down, then park in front of the large lilac bushes, and I would jump out and hop over the cedar rail fence and run over to the log house. I would run to each window and door. All were boarded up, but I still tried my hardest to peer in; desperate to see inside.

    Dad would tell us stories about spending his childhood summers at the log house visiting his grandparents, explaining that we had a long history of our family living in this house and that Moses Hudgin, who built the house, was my great-great-great grandfather. As a young child, this just seemed so astounding. I tried to imagine what life was like back then. I would picture what clothes they might be wearing, and what food they were cooking and eating. I wondered how Moses' whole family – his wife, Ann Mouck, and their nine children – fit inside this small log house, and how they travelled into town? So many questions filled my head.

As a young girl growing up in the 1980s, my only reference for this time period was from watching television shows like "Anne of Green Gables" and "Little House on the Prairie", so of course I imagined myself as Anne or as Laura Ingalls, just not in the prairies or Prince Edward Island, but in Prince Edward County! I was Laura Hudgin of Marysburgh! This fantasy kept my imagination alive with ideas of what life was like for my Hudgin ancestors in the late 1800s, and I kept anticipating our next visit to the log house; hoping desperately each year that the boarded-up windows and doors would come loose and I could just get a peek inside; thinking this would answer all of my questions and give me a glimpse into the real life of our family back then. I still recall a grade school project when we were learning about pioneer life and I, of course, had to write about the Hudgin log house and try to create a model of the house to impress my teachers with.

The years passed and with each fleeting summer visit we watched the log house slowly deteriorate. Eventually, one summer, we returned and the extension that had once been added to the house had either collapsed into a pile of boards or had intentionally been dismantled, yet the doors and windows were still impenetrable! However, my curiosity about the log house and the Moses Hudgin family, and the subsequent families that lived there, stayed with me as I got older, so much so that when I went off to university, I studied history and eventually became a history teacher.

My children now have their own appreciation for the Moses Hudgin log house and their ancestral connection as they are growing up and stopping with me at the house before making our way to the "secret beach". Although the log house has deteriorated even more over time, the history that it possesses and the stories it shares still stand.

The draw to my ancestral land as well as my interest in history have led me down a path to where I am today, contributing to the Moses Hudgin Log House restoration and the decisions on the direction of how this house will be used to educate people about the Hudgin family and early life in South Marysburgh. It only seemed natural that I start to record the stories and the history of the family and of the area, and share that with the public; hence the reason for this book.

Laura Hudgin Edge.
July, 2022

The author, Laura Hudgin Edge, and her father, Glen Hudgin, at the Moses Hudgin log house before restoration, 2019.
[Hudgin family archive]

Acknowledgements

I would like to acknowledge not only my ancestors who have lived in Prince Edward County for over a century, but also the First Nations who occupied these lands over the millennia along with the earth, water plants and animals that have been here long before us.

I want to thank my family, especially my father, Glen Hudgin, who has instilled in me an interest in and appreciation for genealogy and history. I thank him for all the summer road trips down Ostrander Point Road to walk around the log house and walking the nearby shoreline looking for "treasures" and fossils. It is here that I learned how to skip rocks.

I would like to thank my Aunt Bonnie who has always shared my interest in family history, and who has shared many stories, photos and special memories.

My husband Ryan also needs special accolades as he, too, has taken an interest in my family history and has spent hours building my family tree and helping me piece together some of the stories I have been able to tell in this book. My children, Matthew and Julianna, have also grown up listening to my stories, visiting the log house, and have grown an appreciation for their ancestors, and the importance of preserving our heritage.

I have always wanted to write a book about the log house and the history of my family, but it was something I imagined doing once I retired. However, my editor and publisher, Marc Seguin, encouraged me to begin.

A special thank you goes to him for this encouragement, for the deadlines that kept me on track, and for all the work he put into helping make my research and stories flow.

The additional proofreading and editorial comments by Glen Hudgin and Marjorie Seguin are also greatly appreciated.

Heritage architect, Edwin Rowse's comments were integral to understanding the architectural history of the log house and I thank him for his knowledge and contribution to helping ensure this book provides an accurate portrayal of the construction and restoration of the house.

Suggestions from culinary historian Liz Driver were of great help in portraying the types of food prepared and the kithcen technology used in the log house.

I also want to acknowledge Charles Proctor, who wrote the book *200 Years of Hudgins*. It has always been my "go-to" resource over the years to learn about our family history. He was able to preserve and consolidate many of the stories of family members who have now left us. I must also mention Dr. Paul Cole who was the illustrator for Proctor's book, but who is a genealogist in his own right. He has been able to provide me with resources, family trees, stories and photos that have also helped me piece together or confirm my own research.

The motif shown above is engraved on the headstone of Lewis Hudgin (1854-1932), son of Moses Hudgin and Ann Mouck, who grew up in the log house.
[South Bay Cemetery, Prince Edward County, Ontario, Canada.]

Introduction

In 1967, Vernon Hudgin, a great-grandson of Moses Hudgin and Ann Mouck, sold the eighty-eight acres where the Moses Hudgin log house stands on Ostrander Point Road in an area of the south-eastern corner of Prince Edward County, Ontario, that is generally known now as the County's south shore. His reason for selling is debated among family members. Vernon's children have differing versions of the truth[1]. Regardless, 1967 marked the year that the Hudgin homestead left the family lineage for the first time in over one hundred years. Lillian Rose purchased it for $7,000 from Vernon and his wife, Mary, who helped Lillian by holding a mortgage for $3,500.[2]

Since the late 1990s, the Hudgin family have made attempts to purchase the land and log house back from the Roses in order to have it returned to the family (see the letter on page 79); however, they were never successful. So, it came as quite a shock to the family when we learned that the Roses were selling the house, and that a purchase agreement had been made with the Nature Conservancy of Canada (NCC).[3] Two of Vernon's children, Glen and Bonnie, learned of this through a lawyer who had contacted them (as they were the executors of their parents' estate) to inform them that the Roses were selling a piece of the original

---

1 Hudgin Family Memories: recollections of family members collected by the author. Hereafter cited as HFM.
2 Hudgin/Rose mortgage document. See Appendix A.
3 South Shore Joint Initiative. "Historic Log House Restoration," 2020.

property, formally described as "Part Lot 4 (east half), Concession West of Long Point." More specifically, they were advised that the mortgage that Vernon and Mary had held for the Roses had never been discharged and removed from the title. In order for the sale to the NCC to go through, they needed to have the mortgage removed.

The Hudgin family then asked the questions, "Could this mean that our family still owned the property!? If there is no proof that the Roses ever paid off the mortgage and it was in default, does ownership revert to the mortgage holder?"[4] After consultation with their lawyer, it was finally decided that, even though the Hudgins had a legally binding agreement, the potential fight in court would not be worth the cost and hassle as a statute of limitations would most likely prevail. Therefore, Glen and Bonnie went ahead and agreed to the discharge of the mortgage from the title so that the purchase by the NCC could move forward.

The family had some solace in knowing that the property was not reverting to private ownership and that the log house would neither be torn down nor neglected further. Even though it was not going back to a member of the Hudgin family, the NCC assured the Hudgins that efforts would be made to preserve the house. The remaining fifty-five acres of the eighty-eight acre lot, including the log house, is now referred to as the Hudgin-Rose Nature Reserve. The house itself is now being managed and restored by a local Prince Edward County community organisation, the South Shore Joint Initiative (SSJI).

The naming of the reserve to include "Rose" did not sit well with many of the Hudgin family.[5] This was due to the fact that, even though the Roses did own the property for about fifty years, limited efforts had been made by them to preserve the log house. Also, the Roses had severed and sold several pieces of the original eighty-eight acres, leaving only fifty-five acres around

---

4 HFM, 2017.

5 HFM, 2018.

the log house before finally selling that parcel to the NCC. If the Rose family had donated the land instead of profiting from the sale, sentiments among Hudgin family members about the name might have been different. However, to ensure that Hudgin representation would be at the table when making decisions about the restoration, the author joined the SSJI's log house restoration committee and has, since 2021, been contributing to fundraising efforts and participating in the clean up and restoration plans.

This, then, is the story of the Moses Hudgin log house and the Hudgins who lived there for more than a century.

A Note On the Hudgin Name

The Hudgin name has had a few variations in spelling. If you were to add an "s" to the end of the Hudgin name today, you would quickly and passionately be corrected. However, when examining archival documents, you may see spellings ending with an "s", "en" or "ens" and even "eons". This is quite common based on how names were recorded phonetically in the past. The 1863 Tremaine map of Prince Edward County shows Moses' land parcel as Moses Hudgins,[6] yet various census data has it recorded without the "s". In Virginia, where the first members of the Hudgin family settled in North America, the first recording of heads of households in 1783 has Moses' great-grandfather, Lewis, listed as Hudgen.[7] For the purpose of this book, the spelling currently used by the family, Hudgin, will be used except when quoting original documents.

---

6 George C. Tremaine, *Tremaine's Map of the County of Prince Edward Upper Canada*, Toronto, 1863.

7 U.S. Department of Commerce and Labor, Bureau of the Census. *Heads of Families at the First Census of the United States Taken in the Year 1790 – Virginia.* Washington, 1908, p. 53.

Family Tree

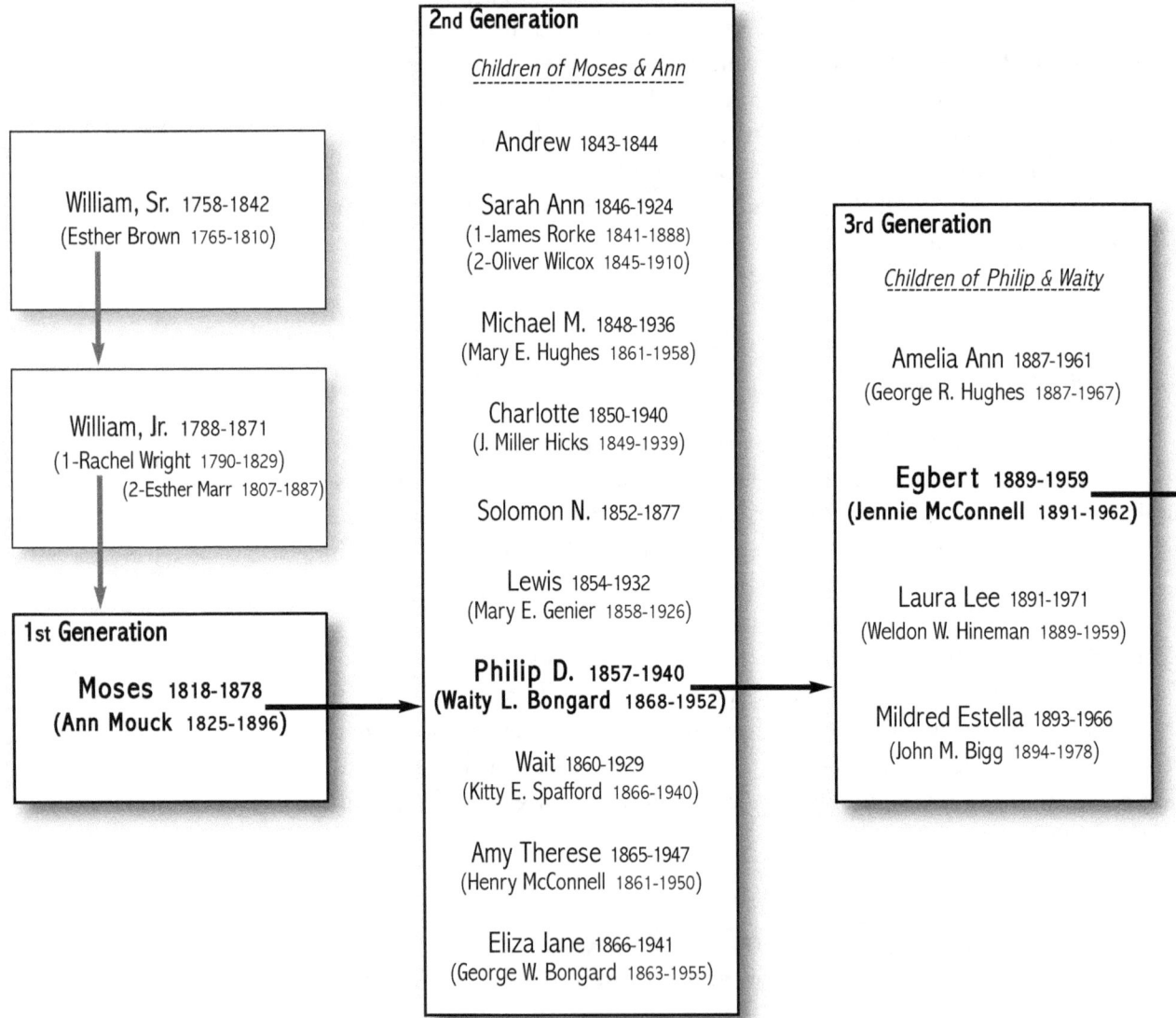

4

Family Tree

Six Generations in the Moses Hudgin Log House

(Hudgin spouses in parentheses)

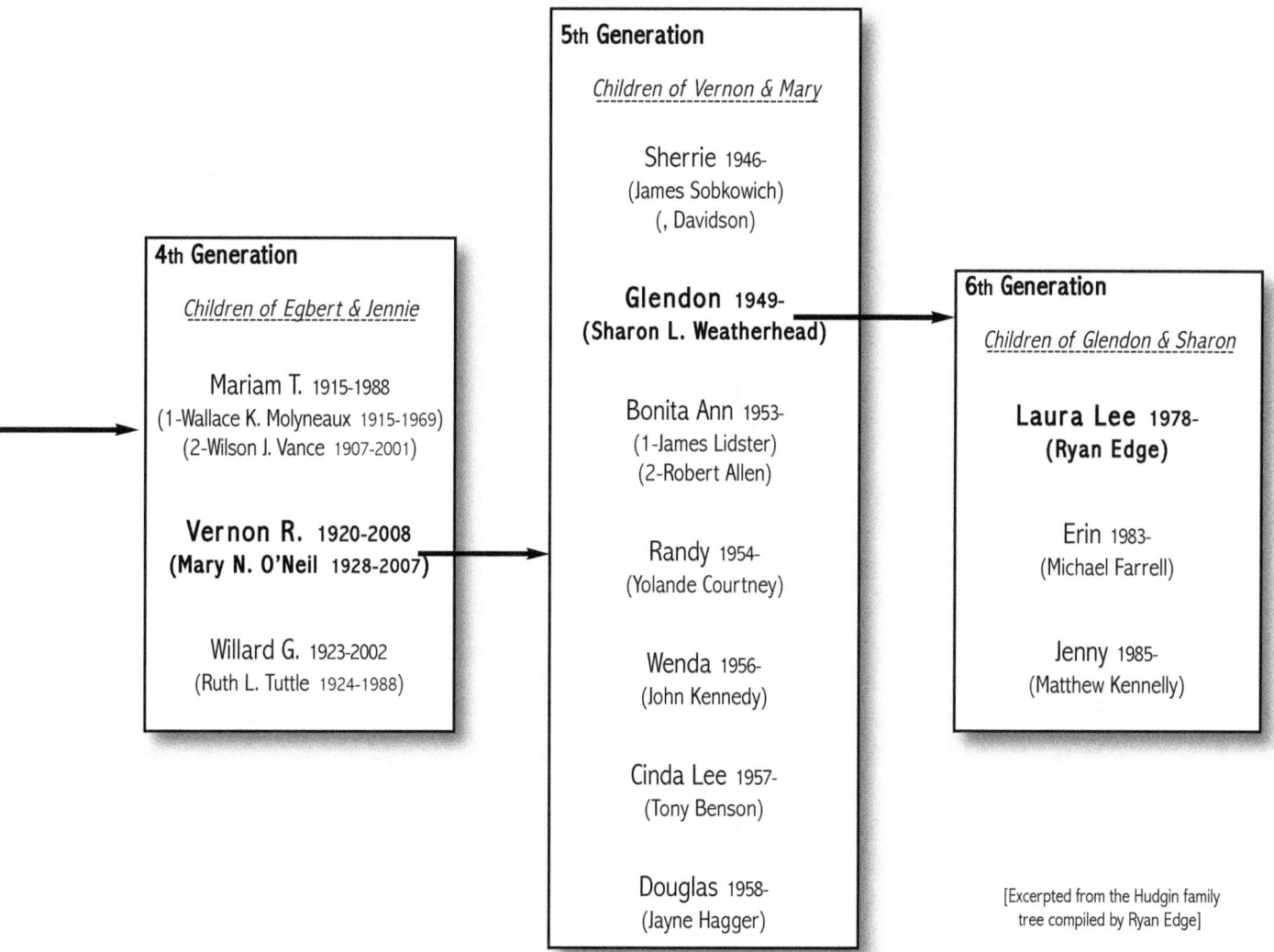

4th Generation

Children of Egbert & Jennie

Mariam T. 1915-1988
(1-Wallace K. Molyneaux 1915-1969)
(2-Wilson J. Vance 1907-2001)

**Vernon R. 1920-2008
(Mary N. O'Neil 1928-2007)**

Willard G. 1923-2002
(Ruth L. Tuttle 1924-1988)

5th Generation

Children of Vernon & Mary

Sherrie 1946-
(James Sobkowich)
(, Davidson)

**Glendon 1949-
(Sharon L. Weatherhead)**

Bonita Ann 1953-
(1-James Lidster)
(2-Robert Allen)

Randy 1954-
(Yolande Courtney)

Wenda 1956-
(John Kennedy)

Cinda Lee 1957-
(Tony Benson)

Douglas 1958-
(Jayne Hagger)

6th Generation

Children of Glendon & Sharon

**Laura Lee 1978-
(Ryan Edge)**

Erin 1983-
(Michael Farrell)

Jenny 1985-
(Matthew Kennelly)

[Excerpted from the Hudgin family tree compiled by Ryan Edge]

The Moses Hudgin Log House

Chapter 1

The Log House

The Moses Hudgin log house is situated in Prince Edward County, Ontario, Canada, on the east half of Lot 4, Concession West of Long Point, in what was formerly known as Marysburgh Township. Marysburgh was originally known as Fifth Town; being the fifth of several townships west of Kingston which were surveyed in the 1780s. In 1784, the name was changed to Marysburgh. Almost 100 years later, in 1871, the township was split into North and South Marysburgh. The Moses Hudgin log house is located in what today is known as South Marysburgh.

In 2011, the Prince Edward Heritage Advisory Committee recommended that the log house receive a designation as a property of significant cultural heritage value (see Appendix B). A combination of architectural features of the house together with 19th Century map references[1] have helped date it. It is estimated that the log house was built by Moses Hudgin around 1860. The building is now designated under Part IV of the Ontario Heritage Act.

Moses and his sons most likely collected limestone rocks for the foundation from around the property and placed them on the bedrock in an eighteen-inch deep trench outlined on the spot where the log house was to

---

[1] The 1863 *Tremaine Map, ibid*, shows Moses Hudgin(s) as the occupant of this 100-acre property. Belden's *Illustrated Historical Atlas of the Counties of Hastings and Prince Edward* (Toronto, 1878), shows M. Hudgin(s) as occupying the same 100-acre lot.

be built. The modest, one-and-a-half storey home was built with seasoned, squared, hand-hewn Eastern White Cedar logs. White Cedars were in abundance in this area of Prince Edward County and, given the size of these logs — six inches (150mm) wide and up to fourteen inches (350mm) deep — the trees used would have been several hundred years old when they were felled. It was a simple construction technique for the time, and perhaps Moses did not have much experience with log house construction, as the corners were lap-joined and not double-tapered (keyed) to lock the logs together as in many other log buildings. Gaps between the logs were filled with cedar boards and then covered with chinking — a hot lime and sand-based mortar mix which sealed the house and protected the inside from the elements. The house had two brick chimneys with corbelling courses and dentil bricks. This was typical of South Marysburgh chimney design but unusual in a small rural building as it shows "much architectural ambition".[2] This detail can still be seen in the existing chimney. Only one

The Moses Hudgin log house, c.1930.
[Hudgin family archive]

The log house is seen here with the original siding and the east wing which was added c.1888.

---

2   Edwin Rowse, "Moses Hudgin Log House Heritage Condition Assessment", 2019, p. 8.

original chimney currently exists; however, the restoration plan includes the repair and rebuilding of both chimneys. The roof was constructed of log rafters, most of which still exist, along with horizonal wood decking boards covered with wood shingles. The shingles eventually weathered and cupped, leading to their replacement many years later by Moses's grandson Egbert and his sons Vernon and Willard. The roof was then covered with tar paper and green rolled roofing.[3] Today, the roof is galvanized sheet metal which was added in 2011 after the heritage designation. A wing was added to the east side of the house in the 1880s and it had a small, gabled dormer protruding from its roof; however, this was removed (likely due to water leakage) when the roof was repaired.

The front window openings are symmetrically placed; one on either side of the south entrance door. There is a window on the east side that is offset to account for the wood stove and its flue. The window on the west side is centrally located. (See plan on page 11.) There has been considerable discussion about what the original windows looked like. However, from viewing historic photographs it seems most plausible that the windows were 2-over-2 sashes. Some of these were later replaced with 6-over-6 sashes as seen in later photographs, including the photo used to designate the historic house. By the 1860s when the Hudgin house was built, this type of window with larger panes was readily available, and two panes per sash was not uncommon. The Gothic Revival architectural style, starting in the 1860s, often included these larger, less divided windows. The upper sashes had arched heads; a detail which would have been "a remarkable refinement in a humble log house".[4] All of the windows were quite large and would have been efficient at letting light into the house. Each also had a storm window insert used in the winter to help insulate the

---

3 HFM, Glen Hudgin, 2022.

4 Rowse, *ibid*.

interior of the house and keep out the cold drafts. The doors to the house were wooden-paneled and still survive today.

The ground floor of the original log house would have consisted of the kitchen and dining/living area. Family members recall partitions between the rooms on the main floor, but it is uncertain whether they were added when the house was first built, or at a later time. The upper floor had two bedrooms and a stair hallway, all separated by vertical board walls.

The wood-framed addition was built onto the log house around 1888. This date is based on a newspaper found between the walls of the collapsed structure (see page 43). It is assumed that, based on the timing of construction, Philip Hudgin built this addition. It was substantial in size and is referred to as the "east wing" or "kitchen wing". The interior walls were finished with wainscoting and plaster that was either painted or covered with wallpaper, some of which has also been found in the fallen debris. This east wing also had a chimney similar to the others and would have been used for the summer kitchen. The wing was accessed from a door at the southeast side of the house, as well as a door on the west side of the addition where many family photos were taken. Based on an examination of photographs collected over the years, this addition fell down or was dismantled in the late 1990s.[5]

At some point, the exterior of the log structure was covered with horizontal ship-lap wood siding, probably very soon after the log house was constructed. The east wing, when it was built, replicated this siding. This cladding eventually fell off over time or was removed, as the logs are now fully exposed.

Around the foundation of the house, there were flower beds that included hollyhocks, and there were wild rose bushes in the front yard. The yard was enclosed by a cedar rail fence that was lined with lilac bushes.

---

5 HFM, Glen Hudgin, 2022.

Chapter 1 — The Log House

The fields surrounding the house were filled with wild strawberries, blackcaps (black raspberries), currants and wild mint. Family members recall the smell of lilacs in the spring and mint in the summer breezes.

The property also has a drive shed that still stands today. It was built, most likely, around the same time as the log house and was used to keep

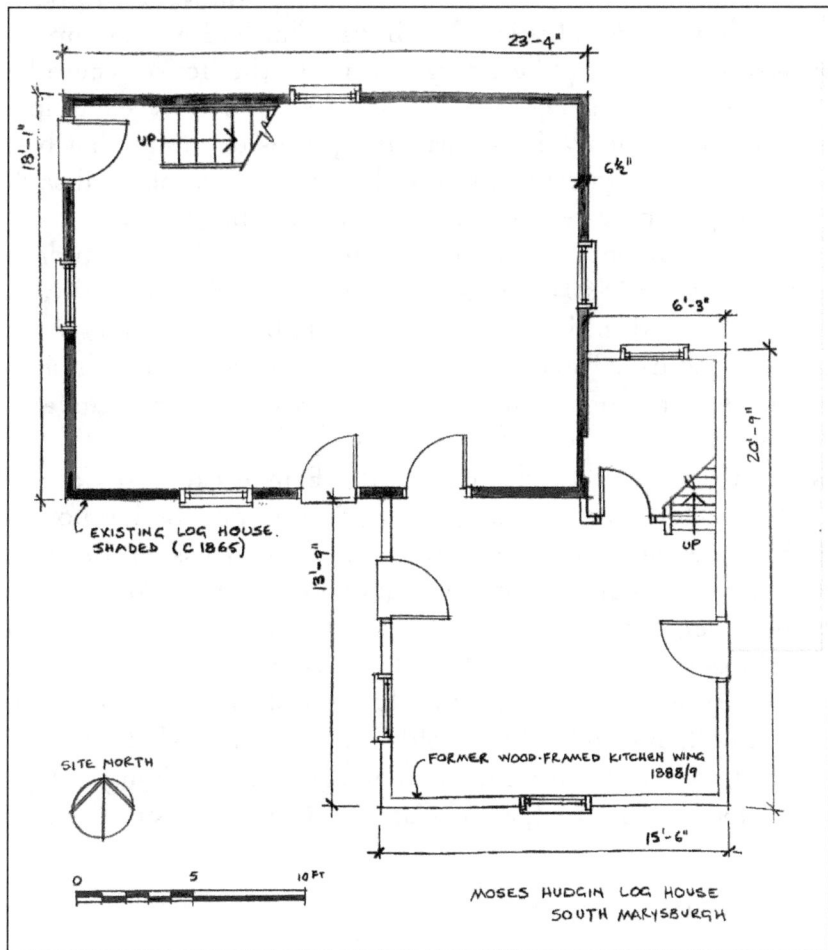

Plan of the Moses Hudgin log house, 2019.
[Sketch by Edwin Rowse, 2019]

This plan shows the east wing (kitchen wing) which was added in the 1880s and demolished in the 2000s.

the carriage covered. At one time, there was a large barn further back on the property that would have housed the horses, cows and any other livestock that the family owned. It was also used to store the hay. In addition, there are remains of a cold cellar (or "icehouse" or "milk house") that was built fairly close to the house, and a tool shed once stood on the property beside the cold cellar. Glen Hudgin remembers his grandfather, Egbert, telling a story of finding an old ship wheelhouse that had washed up on the shore of Lake Ontario, and he dragged it up to the house where he used it as the tool shed (see photograph p. 42). Inside the shed were multiple boxes of nuts and bolts and various parts and pieces of things that had been collected over time. Egbert refused to throw anything out and said, "Every seven years you may need it again or for something else!"[6]

The available documentary evidence indicates that Moses Hudgin built his log house around 1860 in the south-east corner of Prince Edward County on the property described as Lot 4 (east half), Concession West of Long Point, Marysburgh Township. However, it has been difficult piecing together land registry documents to determine when the Hudgin family obtained title to the property.

The first land registry record found in the Prince Edward County archives for Moses Hudgin pre-dates the construction of the log house, and it shows that he owned 134 acres in the adjacent concession. In 1842, Moses married Ann Mouck, and documents show that, thirteen years later, either her father, Michael Mouck (or her brother Michael), sold a 134-acre lot to Moses and then leased the land back on the same day in 1855. That property is identified as "Lot 1, Township of Marysburgh, Long Point or Point Traverse."[7] Moses sold a fifty-acre parcel of this land on April 19, 1859 to Jacob Vandusen, and then sold the remaining eighty-four acres the following year to Harmon Case.[8] One can only surmise that

---

6 *Ibid.*

7 Land Registry Records, Prince Edward County Archives.

8 *Ibid.*

Chapter 1 — The Log House

Moses and Ann lived on Lot 1 until its final sale in 1860 before moving to the property where the log house currently stands, Lot 4, Concession West of Long Point.

Although the 1861 census shows Moses Hudgin living and farming the land on Lot 4, it is unclear if he owned the property. A bit of a mystery is presented in a document that has been uncovered specifying the purchase of "Lot 4, Long Point" for $500 by Moses from his younger brother

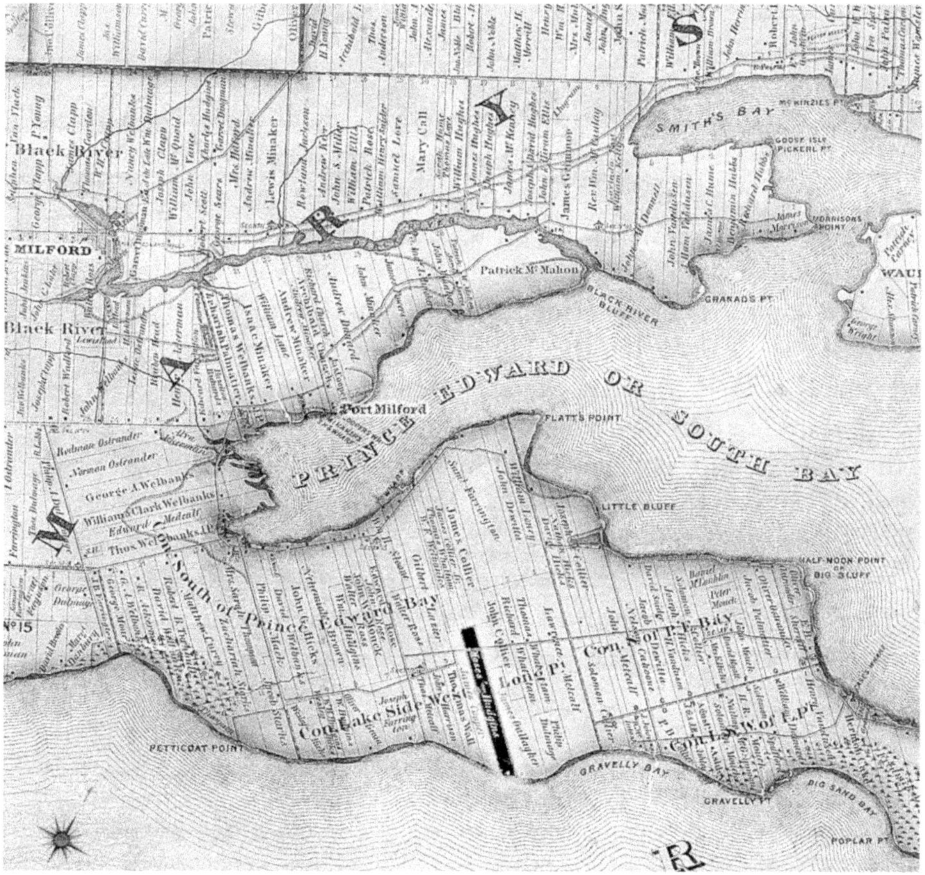

Marysburgh, Prince Edward County (detail), from Tremaine's Map. 1863.
[*Tremaine's Map of the County of Prince Edward Upper Canada.* Toronto, 1863.]

Moses Hudgin(s) is shown as occupying Lot 4 (marked in black at bottom, centre). A building on the lot is shown adjacent to the lakeshore.
The closest town was Milford (centre, left). Port Milford is also shown (centre). The South Bay Methodist Church is just west of Port Milford.

Charles (see Appendix C). Unfortunately, the second page containing the date of the document cannot be located. Where this document fits in to the historical record is, so far, unknown.

The land registry documents located in the Prince Edward County archives indicate that the first transaction for this parcel of land was a transfer from the Crown to Charles S. Wilson in 1881. However, the 1863 Tremaine Map of the County of Prince Edward[9] clearly shows Moses Hudgin(s) occupying the one hundred acre east-half of Lot 4 that extends to Lake Ontario. It is known that, during this early period, the records for land transfers were not completely accurate. Agreements through handshakes and even some written documents may not have been officially recorded. Before 1847, registration of land transactions was not mandatory, so the deed may not have been registered. Abstract indexes were created starting in 1857. Land registrars searched old records to include previous deeds in the indexes, but they did not do so if the deed did not include enough information to identify the lot and concession.[10] Therefore, there may be some errors in the dates that appear in records for this particular parcel of land. Perhaps, Charles Hudgin was squatting on Crown land and, thinking that he owned it, he sold it to his brother. It is also possible that the Hudgins were merely renting the land from the Crown until a patent was issued by the Crown to Charles Wilson for Lot 4.[11]

Curiously, the only building marked on Moses Hudgin's lot on Tremaine's Map of 1863 is located right on the shore of Lake Ontario, more than a kilometer south of where the log house currently stands. However, fifteen years later, the 1878 Belden Atlas only shows a house

---

9 Tremaine, *ibid*.
10 Archives Ontario. "Finding Land Registry Documents," 2020. Retrieved from: http://www.archives.gov.on.ca/en/access/documents/research_guide_231_finding_land_registration_records.pdf.
11 The fourth lot in every other concession had originally been reserved as Crown land. See William Canniff, *The Settlement of Upper Canada*, p.172.

Chapter 1 — The Log House

Map of South Marysburgh Township (detail), Prince Edward County, from Belden's Atlas, 1878.
[*Illustrated Historical Atlas of the Counties Hastings and Prince Edward.* H. Belden and Co., Toronto, 1878.]

M. Hudgin(s) is shown as occupying Lot 4 (marked in black at bottom, centre). A building on the lot is shown on Ostrander Point Road, some distance north of the lakeshore where the log house is currently situated.

in its current location on Ostrander Point Road.[12] Based on the available evidence, it is most likely that Moses built his log house around 1860. Family rumour has it that the original log house was built closer to the water but later moved to the existing spot.[13] It is also possible that both houses were standing at one point, with the log house as the primary residence. Another theory is that a second dwelling, referred to by Charles Proctor as "the Hudgin tenant house", was situated closer to the log house.[14]

Neither physical evidence nor conclusive documentary evidence has yet been uncovered to support these theories. It is interesting to note that the 1861 Census indicates that the type of house Moses and his family were living in at the time, a "log" home, a "1½ storey" house, matches the description of the log house that is standing today on Ostrander Point Road, and therefore it is possible that the house was in fact moved from the lakeshore to its present location sometime before 1878.[15]

---

12 H. Belden, *ibid*, p. 62.
13 HFM, 2018.
14 Charles Proctor. *200 Years of Hudgins*. Toronto, 1976, p. 68. See also Census of Canada 1861, 1871, 1881, 1891, 1901, 1911.
15 Census of the Province of Canada, Prince Edward County, Marysburgh Township, 1861.

Chapter 2

Family Origins

The origin of the Hudgin family in Prince Edward County began after the end of the American Revolution, which saw the founding of settlements of Loyalists, discharged soldiers and Indigenous allies in parts of what is now Canada. One of those settlements became the Township of Marysburgh, first surveyed in 1784 by John Collins, Deputy Surveyor-General, and named in honour of Princess Mary, a daughter of King George III. In the absence of passable roads, care was taken to ensure that as many lots as possible had lake frontage or river frontage in order to facilitate water transportation and communication to the central points of the settlement, as well as providing access for fishing.[1]

Prior to the Loyalist settlement of the region, Indigenous populations were active in the northern portion of the Marysburgh area where there was access to the Bay of Quinte.[2] However limited evidence exists of the presence of indigenous peoples in South Marysburgh. Indigenous history is often passed on through oral storytelling. Written records are limited and archeological evidence is sparse. In the 1700s, the Mississaugas (Anishinaabeg) inhabited the area that later became Marysburgh

---

1 William Canniff, *The Settlement of Upper Canada*. Belleville, 1983. p. 459.

2 John Prinyer. *Looking Backward: Some early history and progress of the Township of Marysburgh*. Picton Gazette Aug. 8th, 1890.

township.³ In 1783, the Crawford Purchase saw the transfer of lands from the Mississaugas to the Crown through negotiated treaties in order to support the settlement of Loyalists and Mohawks (Haudenosaunee). Captain William Redford Crawford reported to Governor Sir Frederick Haldimand that he had "purchased all the lands from Toniata or Onagara River (a tributary of the St. Lawrence, below Gananoque) to the River in the Bay of Quinte within eight leagues of the bottom of the said Bay, including all the islands, extending from the Lake back as far as a man can travel in a day".⁴ By the terms of the Crawford Purchase, also known as the "Gunshot Treaty", the Crown agreed to provide the Mississaugas clothing for all of their families, guns for those who did not have any, some powder and ball for hunting, 12 laced hats, and red cloth sufficient for 12 coats.⁵ To this day, the terms of the agreement are disputed since no actual written treaties or wampum belts exist (other than the recorded, vague letter from Crawford to Governor Fredrick Haldimand). Mississauga oral history has it that they were forced to surrender their rights to all the land within the range of the sound of a gunshot.⁶ This Crawford Purchase paved the way for the settlement of Loyalists in Prince Edward County.

The Hudgin family however, did not settle in Marysburgh at the onset of Loyalist settlement in Upper Canada. Rather, they were granted land in New Brunswick after the American Revolution and settled there before making their way to Prince Edward County. Moses' grandfather, William Hudgin Sr., was a United Empire Loyalist. Originating from Gloucester and Mathews counties in the Virginia colony, William Sr. fought in the

---

3 Prinyer, *ibid.*

4 David Shanahan, "Land for Goods: The Crawford Purchase." *Anishinabek News.* November 8, 2018. Retrieved from: http://anishinabeknews.ca/2018/11/08/land-for-goods-the-crawford-purchases/.

5 Shanahan, *ibid.*

6 "Whose Land." Retrieved from https://www.whose.land/en/treaty/crawford-purchase-1783 .

American Revolution as a sergeant in a mounted troop of Lieutenant-Colonel John Graves Simcoe's Loyalist regiment, the Queen's Rangers, serving under the British general, Lord Cornwallis. After Cornwallis' defeat at the battle of Yorktown, Virginia, in 1781, William was a prisoner-of-war in Philadelphia until 1783.[7] Unfortunately, his brother, Corporal John Hudgin, was killed in action at Yorktown.

William was eventually released as a prisoner and, at war's end, was granted 200 acres of land by King George III in New Brunswick, a new British colony created for Loyalist settlement. William's land grant was described as "East side of the Saint John River 'B' '1' in York County, Southampton, Lot 39, above Mackawie."[8] He and his wife, Esther Brown, began to raise a family of eleven children there — ten boys and one girl — including William Jr., born in 1788. William Sr. sold off parcels of his land in New Brunswick and made his way, in 1809, with his large family to Adolphustown, immediately east of Prince Edward County.

During the War of 1812, William Sr. was enrolled in the Incorporated Militia of Lennox County.[9] As a result of this service, he was entitled to another land grant; however, records had been lost when the American army captured and burned the capital of Upper Canada, York (later named Toronto), in 1813.[10] In 1814, William Sr. and his family moved to Prince Edward County and settled in Marysburgh. He apparently petitioned the government for land in Upper Canada, but without success.[11] He most likely either rented land in Marysburgh or purchased land with the money he made on the sale of his properties in New Brunswick; however,

---

7 Canniff, *ibid*. p. 104. Also see Simcoe, J.G. *Simcoe's Military Journal.* New York, 1844, p. 243.
8 Charles Proctor. *200 Years of Hudgins.* Toronto, 1976. p. 14.
9 Canniff, *ibid*.
10 Canniff, *ibid*.
11 Canniff, *ibid*.

no records can be found of land ownership in Prince Edward County by William Sr. until he was 60 years old, in 1818, when he was granted 200 acres, being Lot 15, 1st Concession South of Point Traverse. However, William Sr. was unable to will this land to his descendants as it was later determined to be clergy land.[12]

William Sr.'s son, William Jr., served alongside his father during the War of 1812 and was also deserving of a land grant, but the records had been destroyed. By 1818, William Jr. was 30 years old, married, with two children. He resided in Prince Edward County and, although he was unable to inherit land from his father, he either rented or purchased his own land. Records only indicate his ownership of land in the County at the age of 58, in 1846, when he purchased the east half of Lot 9, Point Traverse, from John Rose Jr.[13] William Jr. and his first wife, Rachel Wright, had six children, Moses being their second child and first son, born in 1818. After Rachel passed away around the age of 39, William Jr. married Esther Johnston Marr, a 17 year old widow from Ireland. William and Esther had eleven children together.

On October 21st, 1842, Moses Hudgin married 16 year old Ann Mouck, the daughter of Michael (Michael-Eusebe) Mouck and Nancy Ann Collier. Ann was born December 24th, 1825.

The Moucks were among some of the earliest European settlers in Marysburgh Township. They were part of a small group of disbanded German mercenaries who had been hired by King George III to help fight

---

12 Proctor, *ibid.* p. 16. Clergy Reserves were lands set aside in Upper Canada and Lower Canada under the Constitutional Act of 1791 to support and maintain the "Established Clergy" (i.e. the Church of England) in Canada. These reserves, along with Crown Reserves, lasted around 60 years. See Alan Wilson, "The Clergy Lands of Upper Canada," *The Canadian Historical Association Booklet No. 23*. Ottawa, 1969. p. 3.

13 Proctor, *ibid.* p. 48.

Chapter 2 – Family Origins

the American rebels. By 1784, about forty of these ex-soldiers had settled in the region and begun to clear and cultivate the land.[14] After tracing the lineage of Ann Mouck, it is evident that she descended from this group of German soldiers. Ann's grandfather, Gottlieb Mouck,[15] was born sometime between 1738 and 1744 in Unterellen, Germany, and served in one of the Hessian regiments during the American war. He is listed as a disbanded soldier in the 1784 "List of Disbanded Men from the German Troops Settled in Township No. 5, Bay of Quinte".[16]

In 1790, Gottlieb was granted two-hundred acres "On the Peninsula or Point between Lake Ontario and Bay of Quinte, Lot 11, Concession 3".[17] Prior to his settlement in Marysburgh, records show that he was living in Montreal, where he had married his wife Susannah Claus (or Klus).[18] Here, their children Lewis, Michael, William and Peter were born. It is assumed that Gottlieb and Susannah had moved their family to Prince Edward County by 1790 to settle on the land that was granted

Ann Mouck Hudgin, c. 1890
[Hudgin family archive]

Ann Mouck married Moses Hudgin in 1842. There are no confirmed photographs of Moses.

---

14 "Marysburgh Settlement. First Records." Council 1850. North Marysburgh Museum Board. It is also suggested that there were a number of Dutch in this army of mercenaries. However because they spoke German and intermarried, they were most likely recorded as German. North Marysburgh Museum Board, *ibid*.

15 The name Mouck had various spellings as well. Gottlieb is recorded as "Manck" in some documents and then there is "Gotlip Mauk" in the records from the *Centennial of the Settlement of Upper Canada by the United Empire Loyalists in 1784-1884*, Toronto, 1885. p. 210.

16 Library and Archives Canada. "Disbanded Men from the German Troops Settled in Township No. 5, Bay of Quinte, October 4th, 1784." Series B, Volume 168, p. 88. *The Centennial of the Settlement of Upper Canada by the United Empire Loyalists, 1784-1884*, Toronto, 1885. p. 210.

17 Nick & Helma Mika. *The Settlement of Prince Edward County.* Belleville, 1984, *ibid*. p. 233.

18 Dr. Paul Cole, Kingston, Ontario, Canada, colebgp@kingston.net.

to them. Not long afterwards, their son, Michael, met his future wife, Nancy Ann Collier, and they married in 1805. Just three years prior, Michael had been granted 100 acres of land by the Crown — Lot 8, west half, South Side of the Bay in Marysburgh.[19] It is assumed that Nancy and Michael lived on that and, between 1805 and 1831, they had a dozen children there, including their daughter Ann, born in 1825.

Michael's brother, William (Ann's uncle), had been granted 100 acres of the east half of Lot 7, South Side of South Bay in 1803. William Mouck must have prospered as, in 1836, he built a farmhouse out of brick.[20] This farm passed through several generations of the Mouck family until 1981.[21]

By 1860, the year around which the log house was constructed, Moses was forty-two years old and Ann was thirty-five. At this time, they had seven children living with them, with another two yet to be born.[22]

Three years after their first child, Andrew, had died in infancy in 1843, Ann gave birth to a daughter, Sarah Ann (1846-1924). Around 1866, Sarah would marry James Rorke (1841- 1888). James had Irish roots. His father was the first generation to migrate to Prince Edward County. After living in Chicago for a short while, Sarah and James returned to the Milford area in the County.[23] They had one child together, Edward S. Rorke (1867-1939). James was a mariner who saw service as far away as South America and, at a young age, Edward shipped as a cabin boy

---

19 Archives Ontario. Grant to Michael Mouck. 29. October, 1802.

20 Tom Cruickshank & Peter John Stokes. *The Settler's Dream*. Picton, 1984. p. 79.   This was a small house with a steep roof and small windows. In this part of Prince Edward County, building a house with brick was rare at this time. Brick was typically reserved for grander houses in towns.

21 *Ibid*. p. 79.

22 Moses and Ann had ten children, their first son, Andrew did not survive past infancy.

23 Proctor. *ibid*, p. 5.

Chapter 2 – Family Origins

with his father.[24] In 1888, at age 47, James died. Several years later, Sarah married her second husband, Oliver Wilcox (1845-1910), who was an American lake captain. She then moved from the Long Point area to his farm in Cherry Valley in 1906.

Moses' and Ann's oldest surviving son, Michael Hudgin (1848-1936), would follow in the footsteps of his uncle, Captain Ryan Mouck, and become a sailor, spending much of his time on schooners in the upper lakes. Michael married Mary Esther Hughes (1861-1958) and had eight children: Cecil Ann (1879-1982), Charles (1881-1951), Clara (1882-1979), Howard (1884-1979), Donald (1889-1977), Cora (1894-1974), Hilda (1900-1958) and Norman (1903-2000). At age 72, after becoming partially disabled, Michael retired to a farm in Cherry Valley with his wife.[25]

The fourth child, Charlotte Hudgin (1850-1940), would marry John Miller Hicks (1849-1939) on July 19, 1872. Charles Proctor's book states that they lived in the "Hudgin tenant house". This may be referring to another house on the Lot 4 property, close to the log house. Census records imply the existence of this other house by showing that Moses's half-brother, George Hudgin, lived adjacent to the log house. George died of Consumption in 1872 and it is possible that this then became the first home of Charlotte and Miller.[26] Five years after they wed, they moved to a farm they had purchased.[27] Apparently, John was a hard worker and farmed various grains, and raised sheep and hens. Charlotte would make butter to sell at the market. They had two children, William Ira Hicks (1873-1952) and Michael Hicks (1877-1941).

---

24 *Ibid.* p.53.
25 *Ibid.* p. 54.
26 Census of Canada West,1861. Census of Canada, 1871, 1881, 1891, 1901, 1911.
27 Proctor, *ibid.* p. 68.

Sadly, the fifth child, Solomon (1852-1877), would die of tuberculosis, unmarried, at the age of twenty-five.

The sixth child, Lewis Hudgin (1854-1932), would marry Mary Eliza (Marylise) Genier (1858-1926). They had eight children together: Patience Ann (1877-1881), George (1881-1959), Henry Ryan (1884-1959), Emma Luella (1888-1977), Augusta May (1891-1966), Mabel Clare (1895-1896), Erminie (1899-1979) and Mary Louisa (Louise) (1901-1987). Lewis and Marylise may have lived in the "tenant house" after it was vacated by Charlotte and Miller.[28] Marylise, apparently, was renowned for her kindness and good temper according to her granddaughter, Gena Hicks.[29] She was a well-known resident of Point Traverse and would ensure that anyone who visited her never left hungry.[30] Lewis, like many in the family, was a farmer and a sailor on the Great Lakes.

Philip Hudgin (1857-1940), the seventh child, would marry Waity L. Bongard (1868-1952). His life is described in greater detail in Chapter 4.

The eighth child, Wait Hudgin (1859-1929), would marry Kitty E. Spafford (1866-1940) and have seven children: Colin Wells (1891-1981), Leah Delphine (1892-1989), Gladys Geneva (1894-1963), Merle (1897-1984), Euphemia L. (1898-1986), Sarah Colville (Sadie) (1900-1988) and Lucy Irene (1907-1977). In the 1891 Census of Canada, Wait and Kitty are listed as living adjacent to the log house which was then occupied by Philip and Waity.[31] Wait was a sailor and a commercial fisherman, and, at one time, worked on the schooner *Picton*, loading lumber out of Trenton.[32] Wait was also a lighthouse keeper at Point Traverse from 1912 to 1927.

---

28 Census of Canada West,1861. Census of Canada, 1871, 1881, 1891, 1901, 1911.
29 Gena Hicks's memory as told to Donna Douglas, 2022.
30 Proctor, *ibid.* p. 197.
31 Census of Canada West,1861. Census of Canada, 1871, 1881, 1891, 1901, 1911.
32 Proctor, *ibid.* p. 85.

Chapter 2 – Family Origins

The ninth child, Amy Therese (1865-1947), would marry Henry McConnell (1861-1950) and have one child, Percy L. McConnell (1891-1954). Henry spent fifty years on the water as a sailor. He and Amy also managed a farm on Royal Street, Milford, until 1913 when they moved into Picton.[33]

Eliza Jane (1866-1941), the youngest of Moses' and Ann's children, would marry George Washington Bongard (1863-1955).[34] George was a farmer, fisherman and a Great Lakes sailor. He sometimes sailed on the schooner *Picton*, and also worked with the Poplar Point life saving station (also known as the Point Traverse lifeboat). They had three children; Amy Helena Bongard (1887-1963), Lulu Bongard (1890-1945) and Mary Louise Bongard (1900-1999). In 1921, Eliza and George retired to Picton.

In addition, according to the 1871 census, Ann's younger brother, Walter Mouck, was also living in the log house. He was recorded as having an "unsound mind". He died that year at age 40.[35] His cause of death is unknown.

---

33 Proctor, *ibid*. p. 87.
34 Waity Bongard (Philip Hudgin's wife) was the sister of George Bongard (Eliza Jane Hudgin's husband).
35 Census of Canada, 1871.

The Moses Hudgin Log House

Chapter 3

Life on the South Shore

Life out on Ostrander Point on Prince Edward County's south shore in Marysburgh Township in the mid-19th Century would have been arduous. The land was (and still is) mainly composed of thin soils as a result of glacial scraping over limestone bedrock, making farming difficult.[1] Cedar trees were in abundance and the landscape included open and treed alvars, meadows, savannah, woodlands, swamps, marshes, and shrub thickets.[2] Moses and his family were able to utilize what they could from their environment, most notably using the cedar trees as the logs to build their house. In 19th Century Upper Canada, using cedar for log homes was uncommon. Typically, this type of wood would have been used mainly for cedar roofing shingles. However, Moses cut and hewed the White Cedar logs, assembled the log house and chinked the cracks and openings between the logs with lime and sand mortar. This provided a relatively airtight seal, making the one-and-a-half storey house a modest, cozy home that would stand up to the seasonal elements and in which Ann and Moses could raise their nine children.

---

1 South Shore Joint Initiative. "Proposal for Conservation Reserve designation for Ostrander Point Crown Land Block and Point Petre Provincial Wildlife Area." Retrieved from: https://www.ssji.ca/conservation_reserve_proposal_for_south_shore.

2 P.M. Catling, S.M. McKay-Kuja, B. Kostiuk, and A. Kuja. "Ostrander Point Vascular Plants." 2014 retrieved from: https://peptbo.ca/photos/custom/PDFs/Ostrander%20Point%20Vascular%20Plants%20-%208-26.pdf.

In 1861, the ages of their children would have spanned from newborn to age fifteen. The census of that year shows that five of them — Sarah, Michael, Charlotte, Solomon and Lewis — were attending school at that time. There were at least nineteen schools in the Marysburgh School District as of 1848.[3] Presumably, Moses and Ann's children attended the nearest school, the Babylon School house (also known as School #17), located on Babylon Road near what is now Helmer Road. This one-room, wood-framed schoolhouse was built in 1845 and would have been heated by a wood-fuelled box stove located near the centre of the building. One can imagine the long, two kilometer trek to school that the Hudgin children would have had to make; trudging through the heavy, wet snow, carrying their books by hand or held by a leather strap or belt, arriving at the warm schoolhouse and leaving their wet boots, socks and mittens to dry near the stove. In 1867, it was required for each family sending two or more children to school to deliver one-quarter of a cord of wood for each two children.[4] So, Moses would have been making several wood deliveries to the school. The winter of 1869-1870 saw the heaviest snowfall ever recorded, with one hundred twenty three inches.[5] By the time the children arrived at school, they would have needed to hang their outerwear by the fire to dry. The Hudgin boys, Michael, Solomon and Lewis, may have only attended school in the winter, as it was common during this time that boys would remain at home during the growing and harvesting seasons to help out on the farm. By 1871, the other Hudgin children were attending school as indicated in that year's census; Lewis age 16, Philip age 14, Wait age

---

3 Census of the District of Marysburgh. August 25, 1848. From Nick & Helma Mika. *The Settlement of Prince Edward County.* Belleville, 1984. p. 93.

4 Daniel Rainey and Helen Tompkins. *The Educational Tapestry of Athol, North and South Marysburgh Townships Prince Edward County 1800-1966.* Belleville, 2015. p. 195. In 1903, Egbert Hudgin was attending this school and it is assumed that other Hudgin children also went to the same school.

5 Willis Metcalfe. *Memories of Yesteryear.* Picton, 1977. p 23.

11, and Emma, age 6. Their studies would have included the "three R's" (reading, writing and 'rithmetic) with some grammar and geography included. The teacher stood at the front of the classroom and would often have students learn by reciting and memorizing verses and reading from textbooks. Practice work would have been done on a slate and any writing in notebooks was done with a quill pen.[6]

It is also interesting to note that the census data from 1871 indicates that Ann Hudgin was able to read but was unable to write. Telephones did not exist at this time, and even after they were invented five years later, it took many years for them to be widely adopted. Without telephones which could be used to pass on information, people had to rely either on personal visits or leaving cards and written letters, which Ann would not have been able to do. The capability to read but not write may seem unusual; however, looking at statistics from the 1871 Census, we find that one out of every twenty adults in Ontario (about 5% of the total adult population) who could NOT write, were able to read.[7]

Moses and Ann were members of the Methodist Church, specifically the Methodist New Connexion community at South Bay.[8] Methodism was quite popular at the time and had spread rapidly at the turn of the 19th Century. Other denominations of Methodists also existed in the area including the Wesleyan Methodists. From 1865 to 1874, the union of the Wesleyan Methodist Church of Canada and the Wesleyan Methodist Church of Eastern British America led to the controversial formation of the Methodist New Connexion.[9]

---

6   Mika and Mika, *ibid*, p. 183.

7   Census of Canada, 1871, Vol. II, Table X, "Unable to Read, Unable to Write, Deaf and Dumb".
In 1871, in Prince Edward County, those who were over the age of 20 that could not read included 296 males and 236 females. Those who were over the age of 20 who could not write included 295 males and 425 females.

8   Census of Canada, 1871. Their religious denomination is recorded as "Methodist N.C.".

9   Gerald Ackerman, et al. *History of South Bay United Church*. n.d. p.3

The Moses Hudgin Log House

The South Bay Wesleyan Methodist Church (which became the South Bay United Church in 1925 after the amalgamation of four Protestant denominations, including Methodists) was originally built in 1859-60. After this church was destroyed in a fire, it was rebuilt in brick in 1871, at a cost of $2,500, which included a great deal of volunteer labour.[10] An article in the Picton Gazette (date unknown) described the church as a, "...model of tasteful symmetry, with spire and galleries on three sides, aisles and altar carpeted... The pulpit is furnished with a good Bible and hymn book...."[11] The design had an Italianate flair with round Romanesque window arches and a wheel-window at the front. In 1889, the minister, with an annual salary of seven hundred dollars, would oversee six appointments (Milford, South Bay, Hill Top, Carman, Union and Thompson) known as the Milford Circuit.[12]

South Bay Methodist Church, erected 1871.
[From *History of the Churches of Prince Edward County*, 1971.]

The original church attended by Moses Hudgin and his family, burned down. This brick church replaced it in 1871.

Motorized vehicles were non-existent in the 19th Century, so horse drawn carriages and buggies were the primary mode of ground transportation. The distance from the log house to the South Bay church is seven kilometers, and a further five kilometers to the village of Milford. Therefore, a Sunday visit to church or a trip to the general store in Milford would take up to two hours each way. A ride to Picton,

---

10 Ackerman, *ibid*. pp. 5, 12.
11 Ackerman, *ibid*. p. 5.
12 Ackerman, *ibid*.

Chapter 3 — Life On the South Shore

the County seat, perhaps for supplies or a visit to the market on a Saturday, could take three hours in one direction. It was not until 1905 that the first car was owned by a County resident. This was George Farrington (husband of Philip Hudgin's second cousin), who was also the mayor of Picton.[13]

Being so far away from amenities during this time period, it would have been important to be as self-sufficient as possible and make use of the land in a way that could sustain the family. Census data shows that as early as 1861, Moses had thirty of his one hundred acres of Lot 4 under cultivation. He was farming eight acres of rye that produced 110 bushels that year; ten acres of buckwheat yielding 250 bushels; two acres of Indian corn yielding 50 bushels; two acres of potatoes yielding 250 bushels, and 6 bushels of turnips.[14] Moses also farmed hay, but only produced three 16-pound bundles in 1861. The census also indicates that the cash value of his farm was $800, and that the value of his farm equipment was $20. In comparison to other hundred-acre lots in the surrounding area at this time, the yields are on the lower side, as is the value of his farm — many others were valued over $1000.[15] This might have been due to Moses only having just moved to Lot 4 after selling the last eighty-four acres of his property in Lot 1. This may also speak to the poor quality of the low-acid soil that was laced with limestone rocks and gravel which made ploughing and planting difficult. Much of the harvest that Moses took from his farm was likely traded with neighbours or sold at market; the remaining being used to feed the family.

To sustain his family, Moses probably supplemented his farming by hunting wildlife on the property. This may have included deer, rabbits,

---

13 Metcalfe, *ibid*, p. 33.
14 Canada West Census, 1861. Personal Census, Township of Marysburgh, Prince Edward County..
15 Canada West Census, 1861. Agricultural Census, Township of Marysburgh, Prince Edward County.

pheasant, ducks, geese and even squirrels. Recipes from the 19th Century include squirrel stew, which makes one believe this may have been a common meal.[16] Moses would have brought the game back to the house to gut it so that Ann could prepare it using available spices, herbs and fats such as butter or animal lard. Ann would have used an iron cookstove to prepare hot meals. This would have been considered a "newer" technology at the time. In many homes, iron cookstoves had replaced open-hearth cooking in stone fireplaces. The structure of the log house indicates that a cookstove with a stovepipe and chimney had been used.

Women of this time period had extensive experience cooking and preparing meals; they typically grew up helping their mothers and learning by trial and error. Recipes from the time would not indicate cooking temperatures or timing, as this was often based on the type of cookstove or open hearth that was being used. Dora Fairfield, a resident of nearby Bath, Ontario, compiled a cookbook that was published in 1888 with hundreds of pages of recipes. These recipes only listed the ingredients with their amounts along with some basic direction on how to prepare the food. Cooking times were not indicated. Dora mentions at the beginning of her book that, "The management of ovens, the requisite thickness of boiling custards, the right shade of brown upon bread and cakes… these and dozens of other details are hints which cannot be imparted by written instruction, but once learned they are never forgotten".[17] Feeding a family of more than ten in the late 19th Century would have been a feat in itself, so Ann and her daughters surely prepared breads, puddings, cakes, ham, rabbit pie, squirrel stew and more on the iron cookstove in the log house.

Recollections by family members of a variety of wild berries around the property — blackcaps, currants, raspberries and strawberries — suggests that these would have provided fruit for the family from which Ann

---

16 Dora Fairfield. *Dora's Cookbook*, 1888 p. 56.

17 Fairfield, *ibid.* p. vi.

could make jams and other preserves that would last throughout the year. The remnants of a cold cellar are still present behind the log house, as well as old metal caps from mason jars which would indicate this was where food was stored to extend its life. This cold cellar, or "ice house", or "milk house", which were common terms then, was used to keep perishable foods in prior to the invention of refrigerators. It was quite common for County residents to take large blocks of ice cut out from the lake or the Bay of Quinte during the winter and store them in an ice house; insulated with twelve to twenty-four inches of sawdust to help preserve the ice over the summer months.[18] The ice would help to keep the milk cold and perhaps it would be used by Ann to make ice cream as a sweet treat for the kids on hot summer days.

Moses's granddaughter, Clara (daughter of Michael Hudgin and Mary Hughes), reminiscing about her past, described life in the County in notes she wrote. She would have been twelve years old in 1894 when she recalls the eleven-kilometer trip to the Picton Market on Saturday mornings, bringing their packed baskets of butter, fowl, eggs, fruit and sausage to sell. The butter was formed into various-sized rolls that each weighed from one-and-a-half to six pounds. Clara recalls that a large roll of butter sold for about forty-five cents; eggs sold for six cents a dozen; chickens or hens, twenty-five cents apiece; whitefish and salmon, three cents a pound; beefsteak, three pounds for thirty-five cents; stew, five cents a pound, and strawberries sold for three cents for a large box.[19]

Another granddaughter, Emma Hudgin (daughter of Lewis Hudgin and Mary Genier), recalled aspects of life on the farm, especially, "The geese, the bees, threshing time, horse-back riding, milking (by hand), reading by lamplight, home-made bread."[20] Threshing — a method of separating grain or seeds from the head or stalk of a crop — would have been

---

18 Howard Dulmage. *Memories of South Bay.* Picton, 1980. p. 26.
19 Charles Proctor. *200 Years of Hudgins.* Toronto, 1976. p. 58.
20 Proctor, *ibid.* p. 73.

a laborious process when done by hand. If horses were available, they could be used to trample the grain on the barn floor. To thresh by hand, farmers would beat the harvested piles with a flail, which was an instrument with a long tool-handle that had a thicker stick attached to the lower end by a leather hinge. This was called by some, a "poverty club", according to John Prinyer's memories of Marysburgh.[21] John Prinyer was an early resident of Marysburgh for whom present-day Prinyer's Cove, North Marysburgh, was named. He recalls that threshing by hand was a tedious process that could, at best, yield about forty bushels of grain in a day. We know that Moses was growing rye and buckwheat and most likely had to either thresh by hand, or perhaps he was able to partner with neighbours in what was called a "threshing bee". A threshing bee would traditionally be an annual event that took place at neighbouring farms, where the owner of a horse-powered threshing machine would set up at a different farm each day, and folks would come around to help thresh each others' harvests.[22].

Fishing was also an important part of the livelihood of those living along Prince Edward County's south shore. Census data indicates that Moses was not only a farmer, but he fished as well. Lake Ontario provided an abundance of whitefish and, if lucky, large sturgeon. The commercial fishing that Moses likely engaged in involved the use of gill nets, which were particularly effective for whitefish in deep waters.[23] Mesh netting would be fabricated and then sinkers, most likely made of stone, would be attached. They would cast their nets, then shortly afterwards, pull them in full of fish. Moses may have returned to the house with his catch of the day and set up a tripod of sticks over an open fire in order to smoke the fish for longer preservation.

---

21 John Prinyer, *Looking Backward: Some early history and progress of the Township of Marysburgh*. Picton, 1890 p. 4.

22 P.K. Spafford. *As I Remember Prince Edward County and Beyond*. Picton, 1998. p. 24.

23 Suzanne Pasternak. *The Vanishing Legacy: The History of the Lake Faring Families in Prince Edward County. South Bay, Ontario.* Videorecording – DVD, 2014.

Chapter 3 — Life On the South Shore

The rural south shore area where the Hudgins lived would have been considered somewhat isolated, and still is. However, other communities around the County, including the town of Milford, were beginning to expand and grow. Milford, on Black Creek, was considerably closer to the Hudgin farm than Picton. By the 1870s, the town had a population of about 400 people and had many services available including harness makers, shoemakers, storekeepers, cabinet makers, carpenters and joiners, coopers and carriage makers, as well as stores, hotels and a tavern.[24] There was also a travelling peddler who would drive his wagon down various roads in South Marysburgh once a week selling eggs and other produce, making it easier for families living further out to purchase groceries.[25]

Port Milford, on the west shore of South Bay, was about nine kilometers from the Hudgin log house and it became another hub for resources; providing employment opportunities for many members of the Hudgin family. The 1860s saw the growth of Port Milford as a small commercial shipping port where farmers from the area were able to store and sell their products for export to the United States. Docks and warehouses were built for the purpose of storing commodities which, during this period, consisted mainly of barley — an essential ingredient for brewing beer — that would be shipped to American ports. Typically, a sailing vessel that was crossing Lake Ontario to Oswego, New York, would have a crew of three or four sailors along with a cook.[26] Once they arrived on the American side, a tugboat would tow them into port where they would offload, typically, some 12,000 bushels of barley. Over the next ten years, selling and trading barley was a huge asset to the Port Milford community and this period was nicknamed "Barley Days". The ability to also ship other

---

24 Mika and Mika, *ibid*, p. 78
25 Howard Dulmage. *ibid*, p. 170.
26 *Ibid*. p. 3.

goods, such as apples, butter and cheese, contributed to the growth of the region.[27] Moses' brother, Nelson Hudgin, was a sailor and would have sailed out of Port Milford. Recorded memories suggest that Nelson owned the schooner, *Olivia*.[28] It is believed that the *Olivia*, a ship that had been rebuilt at least once, was named after Olivia Hicks of Prince Edward County[29]. Research indicates that Nelson would always store apples and hickory nuts in the forecastle of the ship (the forward part of the upper deck of the ship) as well as russet potatoes.[30]

In 1877, Moses' and Ann's son, Solomon, at age 25, died of Consumption (what we now know as tuberculosis). Life expectancy in the late 1800s was low in comparison to present day. Between 1877 and 1885, life expectancy at birth was at about forty-two years.[31] There are several factors that explain this low life expectancy, one being lack of public health awareness and infrastructure — outdoor open privies often located adjacent to houses, lack of clean drinking water and unsanitary food and milk supply systems.[32] Another reason was the prevalence of infectious diseases. Common diseases at the time included weanling diarrhea[33], scarlet fever, pneumonia[34] and tuberculosis. Of these, tuberculosis (Consumption) was

---

27 *Ibid.*

28 The National Board of Lake Underwriters' *Vessel Register* from 1874 shows "Olivia" as owned by "Hodgins & others". This was likely a typo and in fact it is "Hudgins & others". Retrieved from https://images.maritimehistoryofthegreatlakes.ca/122849/page/86?q=olivia&docid=MHGL.122849 .

29 CHJ Snider, "Schooner Days DCCLVII - Once, 19 Schooners Hailed from Here". *Toronto Telegram,* August 17, 1946.

30 CHJ Snider, "Schooner Days CCXI - Hallowe'en Off Point Traverse". *Toronto Telegram,* October 26, 1935.

31 Larry Sawchuk and Stacie Burke. "Mortality in an Early Ontario Community: Belleville 1876-1885", *Urban History Review.* Vo. 29. No. 1. October, 2000. p. 34. Life expectancy in 2020 in Canada was 81.7 years. "Organization for Economic and Co-operative Development,. OECD Data: Life Expectancy at Birth, 2020". Retrieved from: https://data.oecd.org/healthstat/life-expectancy-at-birth.htm.

32 *Ibid.* p. 34.

33 Undifferentiated acute diarrhea diseases associated with infancy and early childhood are often referred to collectively as weanling diarrhea. Sawchuk and Burke, *ibid.* p. 41.

34 .Sawchuk and Burke, *ibid.* p. 39.

Chapter 3 — Life On the South Shore

the most common disease contributing to mortality at this time. The *Belleville Intelligencer* from February 1881 identified Consumption as the leading cause of death in the Belleville area, and we can assume this was the case for much of Ontario at the time. The newspaper quoted an estimated twenty-six of every thousand deaths in 1879 were from Consumption.[35]

The Hudgin family experienced the devastating effects of this disease more than once. First, with Solomon's death in 1877, and then with the death of his father, Moses, one year later. After suffering with tuberculosis for a year, Moses died on May 18, 1878, at age 59. Ann and her eight surviving children were left to mourn these deaths.

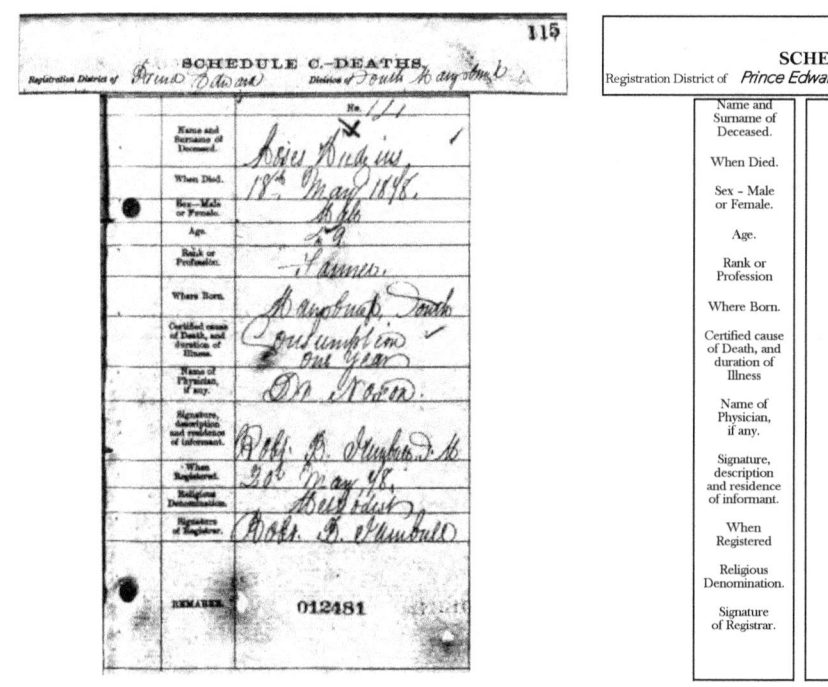

Moses Hudgin Death Record, 1878
(with transcription).
[Hudgin family archive]

35 *Belleville Intelligencer*, February 3, 1881.

The Moses Hudgin Log House

Chapter 4

The Next Generation

The Hudgin family descendants always believed that after Moses died, the house was passed on to Philip where he then raised his family. This may not have been the case according to the Canada census and Prince Edward County land registry documents. Three years after Moses' death, the 1881 census shows his oldest son, Michael, at age 33, heading the household, living in the log house with his wife Mary Esther and their two children, daughter Cecil Ann, age 3, and infant son Charles. Also living with them was Michael's mother Ann, and her four younger children, Philip, Wait, Amy and Eliza.

That same year, land registry documents show that Lot 4 (east half), the site of the log house, was transferred from the Crown to Charles Stewart Wilson. Wilson was a banker and once held the positions of councilor and then mayor of Picton. He was known to have invested in land and rental properties.[1] It can only be speculated that, perhaps, after 1881, Moses's sons, first Michael and then Philip, leased the land from Wilson.

Records then indicate that Wilson's lot, less 12 acres, was purchased by Moses' daughter, Sarah Ann Rorke, in 1893. The 12 acre parcel lying north of Babylon Road was sold to members of the Collier family (the family of Ann Mouck's mother). Sarah had married James Rorke about

---

1 Prince Edward Heritage Advisory Committee. "Barker and Wilson, the Iron Men of Picton. Heritage Walking Tour of Picton Brochure". Retrieved from: https://www.peclibrary.org/wp-content/uploads/2020/04/Heritage_Committee_ Barker and WilsonTheIronMenofPicton_walking_path.pdf.

1866. According to census data from 1871 and 1881, she had been living in nearby Athol Township with her husband and son, Edward. She must have moved back to South Marysburgh after James' death in 1888, as the 1891 census shows her living with her son and his wife in South Marysburgh, and the 1901 census has them living adjacent to Sarah's brother Philip and his wife Waity. The existence of two houses on Lot 4 (east half) has long been suggested by Hudgin family lore. Sometime between 1881 and 1891, Michael and his family moved first to Athol Township and then to Hallowell Township, leaving Philip as the head of the household with his wife and three children. His mother, Ann also remained in the log house.[2]

Detail of Census of Canada, South Marysburgh Township, 1901.
[Census of Canada, 1901. Schedule No. 1, Nominal Return of Living Persons. Prince Edward County].

- Dwelling 85, Family 91
  Rorke, Sarah A. [sister of Philip Hudgin]
  Rorke, Edward [son of Sarah A.]
  Rorke, Sarah E. [wife of Edward]

- Dwelling 86, Family 92
  Hudgin(s), Philip
     [brother of Sarah A. Rorke]
  Hudgin(s), Waghty
     [Waity, wife of Philip]
  Hudgin(s), Amelia [daughter]
  Hudgin(s), Egbert [son]
  Hudgin(s), Laura L. [daughter]
  Hudgin(s), Mildred [daughter].

2 Census of Canada, 1891. Schedule No. 1, Nominal Return of the Living. South Marysburgh Township, Prince Edward County. p. 5.

Chapter 4 — The Next Generation

Census data is typically collected by an agent of the government who would go door to door in a neighbourhood. We can see in the 1901 Census that the enumerator, Henry Wattham, first gathered data at the Collier property. He then proceeded to record information from Sarah Rorke, and then from the next dwelling where Philip Hudgin and his wife Waity were living with their four children.[3] This is further evidence that suggests there may have been more than one house on the east half of Lot 4.

In 1906, Sarah married Oliver Wilcox and went to live with him on his farm at Woodrous Corners near Cherry Valley.[4]. It can be assumed that, even though Lot 4 was in her name, Sarah allowed her brother, Philip, to continue living in the log house with his family.

Born in 1857, Philip Dulmage Hudgin was the 7th child born to Moses and Ann. Although he was not the eldest son (Michael, Solomon and Lewis were all born before him, although Solomon died at the age of 25, in 1877), he was next to live in the log house. Philip, at age 28, and Waity Bongard, age 18, were married June 30th, 1886. Philip and Waity made their home in the log house for more than fifty years. There, they raised their four children, Amelia Ann (1887-1961), Egbert (1889-1959), Laura Lee (1891-1971) and Mildred Estella (1893-1966). They also shared the house with Philip's mother, Ann, until her death on December 10th, 1896, at the age of 70 from heart trouble.

The log house had an extension added around 1889 which was likely built by Philip to further accommodate his family and mother. This date was determined from old newspapers found in 2021 during the clean-up of the collapsed extension. This east wing was a good size (more than 250 square feet, see sketch on page 11) and had been framed in wood and covered with horizontal wood cladding.

---

3 Census of Canada, 1901. Schedule No. 1, Nominal Return of the Living. South Marysburgh Township, Prince Edward County.. p. 8.

4 Charles Proctor. *200 Years of Hudgins*. Toronto, 1976, p. 53.

It is assumed that this wing was used as a kitchen as it also had a brick chimney stack similar to the east stack of the log house. In between the outer and inner walls there was a layer of canvas to seal against drafts and moisture. In this layer were found pieces of two newspapers with a masthead from the *Montreal Weekly Witness* from 1888 and 1889. One piece included an article telling the story of the sinking of the schooner *Blanche* in Lake Ontario off the Cobourg shore.[5]

The kitchen would have been adorned with painted wainscoting and wallpaper on the plaster walls. The wallpaper remnants found in the debris of the collapsed kitchen were a beautiful yellow, blue and white damask print. The wainscoting had been painted various colours over the years — blue, yellow, green and pink. Wood cabinets to keep pantry items and preserves would have lined the walls.

One can imagine Waity cooking on the large iron cookstove; perhaps the same one that Ann had cooked on. Similar cooking methods would have

Rear view of the log house, c.1980.
[Courtesy of the Prince Edward County Archives, HASPE Files]

This shows the east wing before it was demolished. The shed made from a ship's wheelhouse can be seen in the foreground. The ice house can be seen adjacent to the east wing.

---

5 *Montreal Weekly Witness*, June 13, 1888, p. 8.

been used, given that available food sources would have been similar and that horse and carriage was still the main method of transport to access shops or the farmers market. Waity's great-grandchildren recall an old butter churn that used to sit outside in the yard when they were children, most likely left over from the time when Waity made her own butter for the family.[6] One of the great-grandchildren, Keith Hanna, has a vivid memory of visiting the Ostrander Point farmhouse and seeing his great-grandmother, cooking homemade fried cakes (donuts). There always seemed to be a crock of fresh fried cakes in the kitchen whenever the young children came for a visit.[7]

Milford was still the closest community where Philip and his family could find supplies and commodities. However, by 1908, Milford's population had decreased to 300 due to a decline in some of the industries that had made the area prosperous, including ship-building, cheese-making, and the barley trade to the United States. The tariffs that the U.S. government

Detail of a scrap of the *Montreal Weekly Witness*, June 13, 1888, found in the wall of the collapsed east wing of the Moses Hudgin log house.
(composite)
[Taken from a copy at Bibliotheque et Archives Nationale de Quebec]

6   HFM, 2021.
7   HFM, 2022.

had imposed on imported barley by the 1890s led to the end of "Barley Days" as quickly as they had started. Also, the building of sailing ships began to dwindle as steamships, which required complicated machinery, had become a more prevalent mode of transporting goods and passengers due to their greater speed.

According to Howard Dulmage's memories of South Bay, by the early 1900s, farmers who were looking for other opportunities to store and sell their produce came together to build a joint-stock canning factory at Port Milford. To earn some money, Philip may have been able to sell some of his harvest to the canning factory. It is not inconceivable that some of Philip and Waity's children worked at the factory. Dulmage recalls working in the canning factory in 1916 and 1917 for 15 cents an hour; putting pails of tomatoes on a revolving table and taking off empty ones.

Philip and Waity with daughter Amelia, c.1888.
[Hudgin family archive]

Photo: Johnson Studio, Picton.

In addition to farming, Philip followed in his father's footsteps as a sailor and a fisherman. He also worked at the Poplar Point (also known as Point Traverse) lifesaving station between 1883 and 1909.[8] Shipwrecks, including those of schooners, steamers and barges, were numerous in this treacherous area of Lake Ontario.[9] In 1881, a lighthouse was built at Prince Edward Point to

---

8 Proctor, *ibid.* p. 77.
9 Steve Campbell. *Lighthouses of Prince Edward County.* Bloomfield, 2016. p. 28.

Chapter 4 — The Next Generation

assist mariners navigating the difficult waters. It was originally called the South Bay Point lighthouse, later nicknamed the "Red Onion" due to it being capped with a bright red fixed light on the thirty-six foot tower.[10] It was built to help guide ships into Long Point harbour which was known as a safe haven during storms blowing from the west or south-west.[11] Prior to the construction of the South Bay Point Lighthouse, lighthouses had been built on False Ducks Island (1829) and at Point Petre (1833). They were built to guide ships through the dangerous waters of Lake Ontario along the County's south shore. By 1883, the government had moved the original Salmon Point lifesaving station further east to Poplar Point, at which time Philip joined the station with its new life boat.[12] This life boat

Point Traverse lifeboat, c.1900.
[Courtesy Prince Edward County Archives]

Officially known as the Poplar Point Life Saving Station, the Point Traverse lifeboat was stationed in a shed on Long Point, part way between Prince Edward Bay and Poplar Point on Lake Ontario.
L to R, Marshall Spafford, Capt. Leroy Spafford (standing), George Bongard, Willet Austin, David Wood, Jacob Hicks, Philip Hudgin, Daniel Palmatier.

---

10 *Ibid*. p. 29. The lighthouse is also known locally as the Point Traverse lighthouse.
11 Marc Seguin. *For Want of a Lighthouse*, 2nd ed., 2019. pp. 256-261.
12 Canada's first Lifesaving Station on the Great Lakes was located at the Salmon Point lighthouse in Prince Edward County in 1871. The lightkeeper was Moses Hudgin's cousin, Lewis, who was also in charge of the lifeboat there. The Station was later moved to Poplar Point (Point Traverse) where Moses's son, Philip, served. See Marc Seguin, *ibid*. pp. 194-199.

was kept in a shed centrally located on Long Point between South Bay and Lake Ontario. It hung in the shed on swings which allowed it to be quickly lowered onto a horse-drawn wagon for speedy dispatch down to the shore.[13] Numerous marine mishaps gave the crew many lifesaving adventures, often due to strong, gale-force winds. One rescue involved the schooner *F.F. Cole* when its cable broke and went adrift with only the captain aboard.[14] Philip worked on the lifeboat crew under the charge of Captain Leroy Spafford (Wait Hudgin's father-in-law). He also worked with Henry Preston, J.J. Bongard, Marcellus Vorce, Willet Austin, Jacob Hicks, David Wood, Abraham Cannon, Ephraim Palmatier and William Ashley.[15]

As a fisherman, Philip most likely participated in the commercial fishing industry at Point Traverse. In Long Point harbour, there were thirty small boats and three ships officially registered as fishing in this area in 1879.[16] In that same year, records indicate that the catch from this area amounted to 185,000 pounds of whitefish, worth approximately $11,500.[17] The whitefish would have been transported weekly by horse and wagon to the Picton market on Saturdays.[18] One or two weeks in November, especially, could be quite a productive time for whitefish in Lake Ontario, as that is the time that they spawn near the shore. Philip's nephew, Charles or "Charlie" Hudgin (son of Moses' eldest son, Michael) was also a commercial fisherman and he was documented catching a 147-pound sturgeon off of Point Traverse in 1933.[19] Apparently, sturgeon fetched high prices

---

13 Willis Metcalfe, *Canvas & Steam on Quinte Waters*, 1979, p. 153.
14 Nick Mika & Helma. T*he Settlement of Prince Edward County.* Belleville, 1984. p. 83
15 *Ibid*. p. 83.
16 Seguin, *ibid*. p. 258.
17 *Ibid*.
18 Howard Dulmage. *Memories of South Bay*. Picton, 1980. p. 43.
19 Willis Metcalfe. *Memories of Yesteryears*. Picton, 1977. p. 16.

as the fish and roe were considered a rare delicacy and were in high demand from American buyers.[20]

Like his father, Philip often hunted on the property for small game. It was common for him to hunt for partridge, rabbit and especially geese or duck down by the water. Keith Hanna recalls hearing what sounded like a screaming baby at night when visiting his great-grandparents. His grandfather told him the sound was a lynx that roamed the area.[21]

It was recorded by Charles Proctor's mother, Louise Annie Hudgin, that around 1888, Philip turned up at her house with a bad gunshot wound to his hand. They bandaged him and got him to a doctor.[22] Other family versions of the story say it was not a gunshot wound, instead, Philip was injured by an accidental misfire of his rifle while he was hunting and his hand and arm were burned.

Egbert Hudgin handling the fishing nets, c.1920.
[Hudgin family archive]

Like his father, Philip, and his grandfather, Moses, Egbert was involved in the commercial fishery in Lake Ontario.

---

20 *Ibid.* p. 14.
21 HFM, Keith Hanna, 2022.
22 Proctor, *ibid.* p. 77.

Based on an 1897 school photograph showing barefoot seven-year-old Egbert Hudgin with well-worn clothing, we can imagine that, perhaps, Philip's family was not well off. Egbert and two of his sisters attended the Babylon school at that time and they likely used slates; writing with a slate pencil (made of soapstone or softer piece of slate, sometimes wrapped in paper) and using a damp cloth or sponge to erase their work between lessons.[23] Other children whose families could afford it, would have used a scribbler — a paper notebook purchased for one penny. Students whose families were very well off might have a scribbler for each subject. Otherwise, they would have to use a slate which was still widely in use.

Textbooks, too, had to be purchased. Egbert was most likely studying from *The Ontario Readers* (parts 1 and 2), published in 1884, as this was a resource recorded as being used around this time from another pupil

Babylon School class picture, c.1897.
[Courtesy Quinte Educational Museum and Archives]

Egbert Hudgin is standing at far left. His older sister, Amelia, is standing 4th from left, and his younger sister, Laura, is seated at far left.

---

23 Daniel Rainey and Helen Tompkins. *The Educational Tapestry of Athol, North and South Marysburgh Townships Prince Edward County 1800-1966*. Belleville, 2015. *ibid*. p. 192.

Chapter 4 — The Next Generation

who attended this school.[24] In 1884, these books would have cost between ten and fifteen cents, while arithmetic books were twenty-five cents, and geography books were seventy-five cents;[25] considerable amounts at the time. We can assume Philip and Waity's children would have been paying a similar price for their books.

By this time, wood was no longer required to be delivered by parents; rather, the school board would pay the wood delivery fee which, in 1889, was three dollars a cord.[26]

Evidence from early school photos illustrate the fashion at the time and, perhaps, the difference in dress and affluence. An 1897 photograph from the Jackson's Falls School photo shows the girls wearing pretty dresses with puffed sleeves and lace collars as well as "updos" and other fancy hairstyles. The boys have shirts with fancy collars, and some have large bow ties. Older boys seem to be wearing suits with ties, bow ties, watch chains and jewellery.[27] In comparison, the 1897 photo from the Babylon School shows the girls wearing boots, stockings and plain dresses with only a few frills and puffed sleeves, and the boys are wearing shirts with some collars and bow ties. Many of the boys, including Egbert Hudgin, are barefoot and their clothes look a bit worn, likely hand-me-downs, while some of the older boys are dressed a bit better with dress shirts or a suit jacket.[28]

Like their parents, Philip and Waity were Methodists and would have attended the Methodist Church at South Bay. By 1905, the church was in need of repair and a committee was appointed to address this. Through donations and money raised by church goers, repairs to the church were made including re-shingling, a new ceiling being papered and painted, and

---

24 *Ibid.* p. 215.
25 *Ibid.* p. 192.
26 *Ibid.* p. 195.
27 *Ibid.* p. 93.
28 *Ibid.* p. 24.

a new heating source installed as well as remodelling the interior, including new pews.[29] The cost of these repairs was close to $925.[30] It can be imagined that Philip and Waity, along with their children, made the carriage ride to South Bay to attend the re-opening of the church on Sunday, October 29th, 1905. The celebrations continued into the next day when the men worked to convert sheds on the property into a dining room, while the women cooked to prepare a large supper for the crowd in attendance.[31] The celebration not only included a supper but also speeches, music and singing.

As of 1911, the Census of Canada shows that Philip and Waity had only two of their children still living in the log house with them: Egbert (age 22), and Mildred (age 18).[32] Amelia, the eldest, had married George Reginald Hughes in 1906 at the age of nineteen and was no longer living with her parents. Younger daughter, Laura Lee, was also married, At age seventeen she had married Welden Whittington Hineman, in June 1907.

The next census, ten years later in 1921, shows that Philip is still the head of the household living with his wife Waity, his elderly cousin Leyda Mouck (age 78), and his son Egbert and his wife Jennie, along with their two children at the time, Mariam (age 6), and Vernon (age 1).[33] It would have been a very full house! The next year, Moses' daughter Sarah Ann, sold the original lot and log house to Egbert for $300. The deed of land included a provision that stated "and further subject to a life estate in said lands to Philip and Waity Hudgin (his father and mother) jointly or the survivor of them." (see Appendix D) This meant that Egbert owned the farm on Ostrander Point Road, but that his parents were entitled to live there for the rest of their lives.

---

29 Gerald Ackerman, et al. *History of South Bay United Church.*, n.d., p. 8.
30 *Ibid.* p. 8.
31 *Ibid*, p. 9.
32 Census of Canada, 1911.
33 Census of Canada, 1921.

Chapter 4 — The Next Generation

Philip died in 1940, at the age of 82, suffering from cardio-renal disease. Philip's death announcement read as follows:

> In South Marysburgh, Feb. 20, 1940, Philip Dulmage Hudgin in his 83rd year. Funeral service at his late residence, South Bay, Feb. 20, Interment South Bay Cemetery.
>
> After a prolonged illness, through which he was a patient sufferer, Philip Hudgin passed away at his home at Point Traverse, Feb. 20, 1940. Born in South Marysburgh on May 14th, 1857, Mr. Hudgin was in his 83rd year. He was the son of Moses Hudgin and Ann Mouck, and except for a period of sailing days, spent his life in the community of South Bay and Point Traverse, where he was a well respected citizen, good neighbour and friend.
>
> His wife, who was Waity Bongard, survives him, also four children, Mrs. Reggie Hughes, Greenshields, Alberta; Mrs. Weldon Hineman, Toronto; Mr. Egbert Hudgin, South Bay, and Mrs. Milton Bigg, Picton.
>
> He was the last son of a family of eight, but three sisters are living—Mrs. Miller Hicks, Mrs. Henry McConnell and Mrs. George Bongard, all of Picton.
>
> The funeral was held on Friday February 23rd, from his home, and interment was made in South Bay Cemetery. Funeral Services were conducted by Rev. N. Bosko and Rev. R. Babcock, pastors of the Free Methodists Church of which Mr. Hudgin was a member. [34]

Philip and Waity's grandchildren grew up for a good portion of their youth living in the same house with their grandparents. Family memories recall stories from their grandson Vernon about how close he was with his grandmother. She was a short woman and Vernon used to tease her about it. He would joke that she was short enough to walk between his legs when

---

[34] Phillip Hudgin Death Announcement from Willis Metcalfe Scrapbook A. 1986.054.001/A.

he was standing (Vernon was quite tall). Apparently, he was always pulling silly tricks on her and trying to startle her.

Waity's great-granddaughter, Sherrie, remembers Waity as a very small woman and recalls seeing her while she was ill, lying in a bed that looked very large for her size. Sherrie might have been six years old at the time. Keith Hanna recalls her kind, gentle demeanor.[35]

In her last years, Waity lived with her granddaughter, Edna Hughes Hanna (Keith Hanna's mother), who was a nurse and able to take care of her. Soon after Sherrie's visit in 1952, Waity died at the age of 83:

> In loving memory of Waity L. Bongard, widow of the late Philip Hudgin who passed away in North Marysburgh, Monday, March 3rd, 1952, in her 84th year. Funeral service Thursday, March 6, at 2 p.m. Interment South Bay Cemetery.[36]

Waity and Philip at the log house c. 1938.
[Hudgin family archive]

---

35 HFM, Keith Hanna, 2022.

36 Death announcement from the *Picton Gazette* on March 7th, 1952 for Waity Bongard Hudgin. According to her death record Waity was then living in North Marysburgh township.

Chapter 4 — The Next Generation

The Moses Hudgin Log House

MARRIAGE CERTIFICATE

This certifies that
Egbert Hudgins
of South Marysburgh
and
Jennie McConnell
of South Marysburgh

United in Holy Matrimony
According to
the Ordnance of God and
the Laws of Ontario
at Milford
on the 30th day of October
of 1912

Witnesses
Mrs Thos. Farnsworth
Mrs. E. Farnsworth

[Hudgin family archive]

CHAPTER 5

Into the 20th Century

Twenty-three year old Egbert Hudgin married twenty-one year old Jennie McConnell[1] on October 30th, 1912 at Milford, and they moved in to the log house with Egbert's parents and siblings.

Jennie came from a family of cheese makers. Her father was George McConnell who, in 1901, had purchased the Royal Street Cheese Factory located south of Milford, and which operated until 1956. Prior to the purchase, George had extensive experience in cheese production, having previously worked at the Royal Crescent Factory that was a little further east down the road.[2]

Egbert, while young, had become a carpenter. In addition, he worked as a farmer and fisherman like his father, and he was also a general labourer. He made enough money to purchase the log house and eighty-eight acres for $300 from his aunt, Sarah Wilcox, in 1922. As well as caring for Egbert's parents, Jennie would have kept busy in the home looking after the children, Mariam (b.1914), Vernon (b.1920) and Willard (b.1923) who were all born in the log house.

By this time, motorized vehicles were becoming more popular in the County, and by the 1920s, Egbert had a Model-T Ford that had been built

---

1 Many families in South Marysburgh were interconnected. Jennie was the young cousin of Egbert's uncle, Henry McConnell.
2 Gerald Ackerman. *The History of Cheesemaking in Prince Edward County.* Milford, 2001. p. 82.

in 1912. According to family memories, this car had straight fenders with running boards along with kerosene side-lamps and a brass radiator. He later owned a 1924 Buick. Owning a car would have made travel to neighbouring communities much more convenient, especially trips into Picton. The kerosene side lamps even made travel at night possible. Perhaps the family was able to enjoy a vaudeville act or play at the Regent Theatre, which had opened in Picton in 1922.[3] The theatre underwent a remodelling of the facade in 1931, which gave it a more cheerful character.[4] It was owned by George Cook, who died in 1959, and later, by his daughter who came back from Toronto in 1966 to run the theatre.[5]

Although the 1920s saw many technological advancements, such as electricity and running water in many homes, at the Hudgin homestead these amenities were not available. Family memory has it that, at some point, Egbert and Jennie moved out of the log house and took up residence in nearby Milford, presumably to take advantage of these modern conveniences. The exact date of this move is unknown. After the move, though, Egbert continued to farm the land, and the log house was still used, but only as a summer home.

Egbert with his 1924 Buick, c. 1935.
[Hudgin family archive]

3   The Regent Theatre, opened in 1922, had 1200 seats. It once had one of the largest stages in Ontario and included back-drop scenery and dressing rooms beneath the stage See Nick & Helma Mika. *The Settlement of Prince Edward County*. Belleville, 1984. p. 49.

4   Tom Cruickshank & Peter John Stokes. *The Settler's Dream*. Picton, 1984. p. 216.

5   Mika and Mika, *ibid*.

Chapter 5 — Into the 20th Century

Summertime at the log house and Hudgin homestead would have been a nice escape from the modern daily grind of the time, but also a step back to the basics of living. This meant that cooking was still done on the wood-fired cookstove and water was hauled from the well across the road. Jennie's grandchildren remember the woodstove that had a water reservoir, so there was always hot water when the stove was operating. Not a lot would have changed in terms of food preparation at the log house from Ann's time in the 1860s; perhaps there would have been more access to a variety of produce, herbs and meats with the growth of farming and canning in the County. Grandchildren have memories of Egbert and Jennie often sharing a grapefruit every morning with loads of sugar on it! However, gathering local fruit was still a cherished activity — blackcaps, wild grapes and strawberries were plentiful. Strawberry season would see the community get together for a strawberry social at the South Bay United Church (formerly, the Methodist Church), where Egbert and Jennie would attend with their children and, eventually, their grandchildren. Egbert's grandson, Glen, recalls the smell of Grandma Jennie's fruit pies and her making ice cream as a treat for the grandkids in the summer. He remembers how creamy and buttery it was and such a sweet delight on a hot summer's day.

Egbert and Jennie's children attended the Port Milford School (SS #13 South Marysburgh, situated adjacent to the South Bay Methodist church).[6] It was common that students only attended school up until grade eight, especially rural or "farm kids", and we know this was the case for Vernon Hudgin.[7] The original log schoolhouse, built in 1855, was replaced five years later by the present masonry building which is still standing. By the time the Hudgin children were attending the school,

---

6 Rainey, and Tompkins, *Educational Tapestry of Athol, North and South Marysburgh Townships* p. 199.
7 HFM, 2021.

several repairs and updates had been effected, including a new maple floor in 1922 that cost $88.[8]

By the 1930s, music had become an important part of the education curriculum, and music teachers were hired to travel from school to school delivering a music program.[9] The Hudgin children would have been attending school when a new organ was purchased in 1929, as well as a new slate blackboard for the front of the classroom.[10] The itinerant music teacher in 1936 was E.H. Smith, and he earned $50 per annum.[11] An organ that had been given to Jennie and Egbert's granddaughter was removed from the log house when it was sold in 1967, so perhaps the Hudgin children were able to practice and play the organ in the house.

A popular game the Hudgin children likely played in their school years was "Fox and Geese", common in the winter when the kids could draw a fifty-foot circle in the snow with a centre spot for the fox, and paths like spokes of a wheel, radiating outward. The kids would tag someone to be the fox as the others would run along the paths as the geese, avoiding the fox.[12]

In the late 1930s, apparently, the Babylon schoolhouse was used by the army as a bunkhouse while they were clearing the land on the south side of Babylon Road.[13] In 1938, the Department of National Defence had purchased several parcels of land in the County for training purposes. This included the lot at Ostrander Point directly across the road from the log

---

8 Rainey and Tompkins, *ibid*. p. 195.

9 *Ibid*. p. 198.

10 *Ibid*. p. 195.

11 *Ibid*.

12 P.K. Spafford. *As I Remember Prince Edward County and Beyond*. Picton, 1998. p.53.

13 By 1938, the school was no longer in operation. In the early 1960s, it was sold and moved off site. See Rainey and Tompkins, *ibid*, p. 215.

house (still Crown land today). This land was used for firing, bombing and target practices during World War II. This resulted in many spent cartridges left lying around the property, and even some unexploded explosive ordnance (UXO).[14] As a child, Vernon's son, Glen, recalls seeing old brass cartridges sitting under the washbasin at the back door while visiting his grandparents; most likely collected over the years after the military training site had been abandoned.

In July of 1940, a year after the outbreak of World War II, Vernon, at age 20, joined the Canadian Army and began his active service at Kingston two years later. There are a few photos of Vernon in his uniform standing outside of the log house before he was shipped overseas.

After basic training in Cornwall, Ontario, and advanced training at Camp Borden, he was transported overseas with his fellow soldiers on the troopship *RMS Andes* departing from Halifax, Nova Scotia, disembarking at Greenock, Scotland.[15]

Vernon at the farm, ready to be shipped overseas during WWII.
[Hudgin family archive]

---

14 Canada Department of National Defence. "Practicing UXO safety in Prince Edward County, Ontario, 2017." Retrieved from: https://www.canada.ca/en/department-national-defence/services/uxo/uxo-locations/practicing-uxo-safety-prince-edward-County.html.

15 HFM.

Jennie wrote many letters to Vernon during his time in training and while he was overseas. One way she was sending letters was through Airgraph, a technology that allowed letters to be photographed on small rolls of film which were then sent overseas. This technology saved space when transporting thousands of letters and allowed for quicker delivery. The letters could then be projected or printed for viewing.[16]

Vernon was a member of the Hastings and Prince Edward Regiment (the Hasty P's), in the 16th Platoon of "D" company, stationed at Eastbourne on the English Channel coast. He participated in training exercises in North England, Inveraray and Darvel, Scotland. In 1943, the regiment embarked aboard the *Duke of Argyll*, bound for the Mediterranean Sea to invade Sicily. On the way, Vernon wrote a letter home to his parents:

My Dearest Mother and Father;

Before I write very much I don't want you to shed any tears over this letter. As I write I am somewhere in the Atlantic and this is my last chance to write before we go into action. The time has come when the Canadians must see action and a lot of us will have to give our lives and if I am among those, dearest parents, I don't want you to worry or weep because it will be God's will and not ours. I am not afraid to die because I know it will be for a good cause. You will probably see in the paper or hear over the radio where this raid will be.

You will never know how hard it is to write this letter for I don't know what to write but I love you both better than life itself. There have probably been times when you thought I was against you, but never. I'll never forget when I told you I was on draft for overseas. You don't know what it cost me to tell you that.

---

[16] Letter from Jennie to Vernon, March 11th, 1943. See also, James Montagnes. "Mail in Miniature." *MacLean's Magazine*. September 15, 1943. Accessed from: https://archive.macleans.ca/article/1943/9/15/mail-in-miniature.

I don't want you to give up hope even if you hear I am among the missing. You must remember there are fathers and mothers all over the world mourning over their sons. Don't give up hope until you are positive I am dead.

Well, dearest father and mother it's costing me a lot (emotionally) to write this letter but you must always remember God's Will is His Will and if I am spared you'll never see a happier son coming home than me.
Well, I will close now leaving the matter in God's hands.

Ever your loving son.

Vernon XX [17]

Vernon sustained serious wounds during an enemy artillery barrage on July 23rd, 1943, only 13 days into action. He ended up being transported to the 95th British General Hospital at Algiers, Algeria, where the treatment for his wounds and subsequent infections involved removing parts of his stomach and intestines. In the fall of 1943, once he was well enough to walk, he was shipped back to England. In March 1944, he was finally released from hospital and returned to Canada, arriving in Halifax, Nova Scotia, in April 1944, right around his 24th birthday on April 13th. Recovery was ongoing even after he returned home. Vernon was an outpatient at the Kingston Hospital for another month as more shell fragments

---

17 Letter, Vernon Hudgin to Egbert and Jennie Hudgin. Hudgin family archive.
At age 85, several months after returning home from the Hasty P's reunion trip to Sicily in September 2005, Vernon was house cleaning with his daughter, Bonnie, when she found an old photo of him in his army uniform and placed it on his nightstand. She noticed that the photo seemed to be crooked in the frame, so she took the back off to straighten it. Behind the backing was the letter Vernon had written to his parents in 1943 while in transit to Sicily. Vernon thinks his mother must have put the letter behind the picture all those years ago, but he never knew it was there.

were removed and the continued infection was dealt with. Vernon received a medical discharge from the Canadian Army at the end of June 1944,[18] yet the injuries affected him for the rest of his life.

When Waity, Vernon's grandmother, wrote him a letter on August 11, 1943, she was most likely unaware that he had already been wounded. She talks about how it is hard to tell there is a war going on with the number of cars she sees in Picton but food is being rationed and fruit is scarce to find. "Milt and Harold went back picking huckle berries and made $50, selling them at $1.60 a six quart basket". At the time, sugar was rationed at two pounds a month.[19]

While Vernon was overseas, Egbert and Jennie relied on his younger brother, Willard, who, at the age of 18 by 1941, helped out around the log house and farm. According to a letter Jennie wrote to Vernon while he was still training in Canada, Willard was responsible for taking the cows down to the lake for water and also helped to harvest the hay:

> South Bay, Ont.
> July 3rd, 1941
>
> Dear Vernon,
>
> We received your letter last night and was glad to hear you got there all right. Dad went to work this morning and Willard has just gone to the lake with the cows he was out to Geraldine's this morning. It is 15 minutes after nine, we took the calves Monday Egbert didn't go to work till afternoon we went to the stock yards and Willard and I went on to Leone's. I gave Geraldine your address and she is going to write to you; our two calves weighed 4.00 and something. They came to $36.75 cents and the other $19.45! I was talking to Rosie last night on the phone and

---

18 HFM.
19 Waity Hudgin to Vernon Hudgin, Hudgin family archive.

she said she got a letter from Ivan   how is Carmon getting along, I haven't seen any of Mervins since Sunday.

Is it as nice a camp as Petawawa, someone said there wasn't many shade trees. Lyall Minaker brought his car home Monday night. It's a nice car. If we had one like it we could come down and see what your camp looks like. Jack ?--? is coming Sunday and bringing Rex Walters mother. I think it would be quite a long drive. It is so cold here to-day. I have to keep a fire and yesterday was so warm we had to keep the doors all open. There must of been a storm somewhere.

Willard is drawing in the hay. Keith Bedbourgh came down this morning and he is helping. We just had our dinner. Willard is playing the radio. He is waiting for me to get this finished so he can take it to the mailbox. So I will have to close. I don't know any news to write. Maybe I can write more next time.

With love from Mother and Dad.
P.S. Willard will write next time.[20]

In this letter, Jennie mentions Willard listening to the radio. Even though the house did not have electricity, the family most likely had a radio for a number of years that was battery operated. A few decades prior to 1941, advertisements for radios were quite common in the newspapers. They offered a way to hear music and conversations from far away locations. By 1921, there were quite a few broadcasting stations that could be tuned into and, by 1930, several commercial radios were available from such companies as Deforest Crosley, General Electric, Magnavox, Northern Electric, Marconi, and others.[21] By this time, even sporting events were being broadcast and provided great entertainment for many of the men.

While Vernon was still overseas, Willard had reached the age of 20 in 1943, and married Ruth Tuttle that year. They had their first son Floyd

---

20 Letter, Egbert and Jennie Hudgin to Vernon Hudgin. Hudgin family archive.
21 P.K. Spafford. *As I Remember Prince Edward County and Beyond*. Picton, 1998. p. 34.

in 1944, followed by Terry (b. 1946), Eric (b. 1947), Carol (b. 1948), Ronda (b. 1949), and Eunice (b. 1951). Willard later became a licensed mechanic, following the same career path that his brother, Vernon, would take after returning home from the war.

Vernon's cousin, Margaret Collier, had written to him while he was overseas in 1943 and explained how she was working at Benson's canning factory in Cherry Valley. A whole truck-load of people from Milford would be driven to the factory. Margaret explains it as being "packed in like sardines". They peeled tomatoes at the factory and would be paid seven cents a pail plus two cents bonus on every dollar. They would have to pay twenty cents just for the transportation to get there. Margaret also mentions having gone to two "shows" lately, probably at the Regent Theatre in Picton. She saw "The More the Merrier" and "Happy Go-Lucky", which was in "technicolor".[22]

Vernon, Mariam and Willard at the log house, c.1940.
[Hudgin family archive]

22 Letter from Margaret Collier to Vernon Hudgin, 1943. This and subsequent references in this chapter are HFM or from the Hudgin family archive. Margaret Collier was Vernon's older first cousin. Her mother was Ella Ann McConnell Collier, sister of Vernon's mother, Jennie.

Mariam (Willard and Vernon's sister) was known as a very kind, gentle and giving soul. She had contracted polio as a young woman and wore braces on her legs and, later in life, had to use a wheelchair. Although Mariam could not use her legs, she was still able to drive as she had a car modified so that she could change gears and use the brakes with hand controls. She married Wallace Molyneaux and had two children, Gary (b. 1942), and Neil (b. 1946). They lived on a farm on Ridge Road just outside of Picton. Wallace died from a heart attack in 1969. Their son, Neil, passed away at the age of 29 in 1975 when a plane he piloted crashed while flying over their property in South Marysburgh. Due to her disability, Mariam did not work outside the home but was known as an amazing wife, mother, aunt and sister. She would scoot around on a special wheeled chair that was made for her, and do her ironing, cooking, baking and cleaning. Nothing seemed to faze her, and she was always there for anyone who needed her. Mariam remarried later in life to Wilson Vance, known as "Wilse" by close family.

Egbert and Jennie's grandchildren have fond memories of visiting their grandparents at the log house when they were young. Willard's son,

Egbert and Jennie with their daughter Mariam, c.1940.
[Hudgin family archive]

Terry, recalls pulling up to the house for a visit and always finding Jennie and Egbert sitting on an old wooden church pew underneath the oak tree. Vernon's son, Glen, remembers being responsible for fetching the water for the family from the dug well across the road. He would have to take the cover off the well, while checking for snakes nearby. He would then take the metal pail and swish it around the water at the top of the well to clean the floating debris away before dunking the pail in and pulling up the fresh water. He would carry it back to the house and place the bucket on the stove. Anyone who wanted a drink would take the black-handled dipper and swish it around to get the wrigglers (mosquito larvae) out of the way and then dip it at the right time to get a clean drink of water — without wrigglers!

Across from the well was the drive shed. Glen and his sister, Wendy, remember being told by their parents and grandparents not to play in it. However, from time to time, they would sneak in to explore. They recall seeing a horse-drawn sleigh and carriage that were housed in the shed that, most likely, had belonged to their great-great grandfather, Moses. There were also boxes of car parts, leather straps hanging from the wall and, of course, bats, which had taken up residence there. Behind the drive shed was the household rubbish pile. The kids would dig in the pile for fun and would find little treasures such as tiny medicine bottles; also pieces of clay pipes and broken dishes.

The log house had a small space partitioned off under the stairs on the main floor that created a tiny room with a door. The north side window allowed light to enter this space. There was a small writing desk in this room and it was referred to as the writing room. There was empty space directly under the stairwell that the grandchildren called the "cubby hole". Willard's son, Terry, remembers a few of the kids getting stuck in there one time and Egbert having to get them out.

There was an old ladder-back rocking chair on the main floor that many family and visitors would sit in. One day, Terry and his brother Eric decided

Chapter 5 — Into the 20th Century

to get on the back and stand on the rungs. They ended up snapping the chair in half. They panicked with fear that they would get in trouble from their grandfather, but Egbert did not really say much. Family memories tell of Egbert being a mild-mannered, gentle soul who rolled his own cigarettes and also smoked a pipe and cigars. Terry still has that same chair today. He fixed it by replacing the rungs and weaving a new seat out of rope.

Terry also remembers his dad helping his grandfather put shoes on the horses by the barn (which no longer stands today). The horses' hooves would have iron shoes nailed on with square nails that would then get bent over and broken off. The hooves were then chiseled all the way around and the rough edges would be smoothed with a file. The hooves were then put up on a block of wood and the square nails would get trimmed. Many

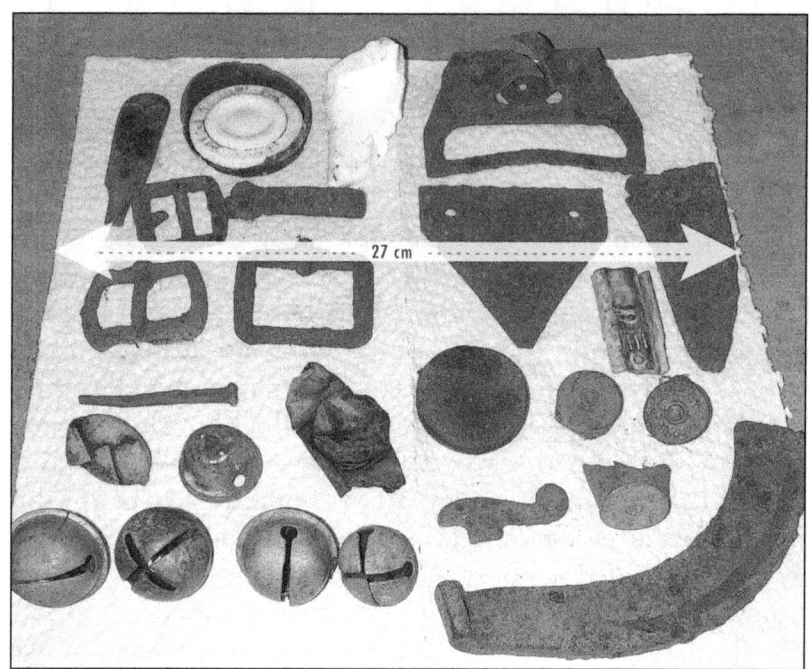

Artefacts unearthed at the Moses Hudgin log house, 2021.
[Metal detecting and photo courtesy of Kevin Flynn, 2021.]

Using a metal detector, several items were found around the log house: Spoon or fork handle (upper left), three harness buckles, a square-head nail, sleigh bells, part of a horseshoe (lower right), three bases from spent cartridges used in the wing cannon of an RCAF aircraft, various unidentified objects. (27cm scale added for clarity)

of these nails have been dug up after being found with a metal detector in and around the property, along with horse and sleigh bells that may have dated back to Moses' and Ann's time.

The grandchildren visiting in the summer could find themselves bored from time to time. One way of occupying themselves was by pulling the horse buggy down to the lake and back; just for something to do. Egbert tried to entertain his grandchildren in various ways. He built them a swing out of wooden poles that had washed up on shore, most likely from an old ship. There are also memories of Egbert whittling many things out of wood, including hand-held windmills with a stick and a wooden blade so the children could run with them and watch the blades spin. Glen has a jack knife that he received as a gift from his grandfather. He always imagined whittling wood just like Egbert used to do.

One of Terry's most vivid memories is watching his dad and grandfather pull the wagon into the barn and unload loose hay to store. The pitchfork they used was the big kind with the handle that locked the hay in, which made it easier to slide and release. He recalls the many hours the family would put into preparing the hay. At one point, a huge windstorm blew the barn down.

Glen recalls that, when visiting his grandparents, he kept busy with a small, handmade parachute with a weight (most likely a rock) attached to it that his dad made out of fabric found in his dad's war chest. He would throw the tiny parachute up in the air and watch it fall to the ground. There was also a wagon-wheel toy that Wendy and Glen remember their dad and grandfather building using the outer metal rim of the wooden wagon wheel and a wire loop with a wooden fishing-net float as a handle. The kids would run around the property with it trying to keep it upright and steering it in various directions and up and over obstacles. Apparently, this would entertain the kids for hours. Glen recollects playing hide and seek, touch tag and other games, but much of their time was spent exploring. "We would all go down to the lake together to go swimming and we would often picnic there. I remember standing on the running board of grandpa's car to get down to the lake." Another one of Glen's memories included riding with a bunch of his cousins in the back of his uncle Willard's red pickup truck when he imagined that if he jumped up high enough out of the truck, he should be able to land on his feet and just keep running alongside. Well, that little experiment did not work out well for him and he ended up pretty bruised and bloody. His biggest concern, though, was the rips and tears he got in his clothes!

Glen also remembers celebrating his ninth birthday at the house. His grandfather, Egbert, pulled him aside and gifted him a small, porcelain dog that looks like a Staffordshire figurine of a spaniel which his grandfather said he had found when he was nine years old. To Glen, this was such a meaningful gift. He cherished that dog and still has it today; always searching for its match to make it a pair whenever he visits antique shops.

Out in the back field behind the house was an old, abandoned car; a rusted relic that Glen and Wendy remember playing on as children and pretending to drive while sitting in the driver's seat. The property had lots of milkweed and butterflies, especially many monarchs. The kids would pick the dry milkweed pods, releasing the silky seeds into the breeze. Memories of common birds that were seen frequently at the property included catbirds, bobolink, killdeer and snipes. Keith Hanna remembers hearing the distinct call of the whip-poor-will. Egbert and Jennie's grandchildren remember the smell of the wild mint growing at the front of the property. The aroma would fill the air, and they would often pick the leaves for a stronger sniff. The lilac bushes in front of the house also hold a lot of memories for many of the children as well. Wendy recalls climbing inside the bushes to a small cleared-out space to create a fort, and the kids would hide in there and play.

Porcelain dog figurine.
[Photo: Glen Hudgin, 2022.]

Found by Egbert in 1898, and gifted to his grandson, Glen, in 1958.

The Moses Hudgin Log House

The property across the road that was owned by the Department of National Defence (DND) continued to be used for various training purposes over the years. There was an old lookout tower across from the log house that belonged to DND. Terry remembers his younger brother, Eric, trying to be brave by climbing it, but when he got to the top he froze with fear, so several of the kids ran over to help get him down. The planes from the Airforce often flew over the property with red targets towed behind them. One day, when a target fell to the ground, Terry ran over with Eric and picked it up. They sold it to Vernon for ten dollars and he used it to make car seat covers for a 1956 Pontiac!

One week in the spring, Willard's oldest boy, Floyd, had stayed over at the house with his friend Roland Pounder. Just for fun, they decided to build a boat out of wood they found around the property. The boat leaked so badly they brought it back from the shore and put tin on the bottom with about 300 roofing nails. They attempted to take it out in the lake again but there were so many holes from the nails, the boat just sank!

Nine of Egbert's and Jennie's grand-children at the log house, c. 1955.
[Hudgin family archive.]

Chapter 5 — Into the 20th Century

Vernon's daughter, Bonnie, remembers when she would visit in the summer. She would sleep upstairs in the log house but had a constant fear of bats. She can still recall the smell of the bats; most likely from the guano. Terry tells a story of a bat getting stuck in Sherrie's hair and Aunt Mary had to cut it out. Sherrie confirms this story and remembers it well.

As Egbert and Jennie got on in years, they made the decision to move from Milford into Picton while still keeping the log house as a "summer home" where the rest of the family could continue to visit. They moved into a small brick house on Main Street which has long since been demolished.

Egbert passed away on January 10th, 1959, from emphysema, most likely caused from smoking over the years. He was 69 years old.

When Jennie got sick, she moved in with her daughter, Mariam, on her farm outside of Picton, where they had set up a bed in the downstairs living room. Jennie passed away on June 28th, 1962, at the age of 72.

The Moses Hudgin Log House

CHAPTER 6

The Last Generations[1]

Vernon returned to civilian life after his service in World War II. He became a licensed mechanic through a government rehabilitation training program. Vernon met his wife, Mary Nita Murney O'Neil, shortly after his return from the war. Mary was from the Glenora area of Prince Edward County, on the Bay of Quinte. Her family originated from Ireland. Apparently, Vernon and Mary had gone on a double date arranged through friends; however, Vernon was not supposed to be meeting Mary, but rather the other girl, and Mary was supposed to be with the other gentleman. Yet, the "other" two seemed to get along better and they ended up changing their minds about who was with whom. Mary and Vernon's daughter, Bonnie, remembers them telling stories about how the other two were, "…making out in the back seat of the old car while they sat in the front and talked."

Vernon was older than Mary by eight years, according to their birth certificates, even though Mary always claimed that hers was off by one year. When Vernon asked her to marry him, she was not of legal age and she apparently forged her guardian's signature on the marriage application because she was only seventeen and needed to be eighteen to get married. They were married December 17th, 1945, and on that day there was a huge snowstorm! Vernon got his old car, a Durant, stuck in the deep snow near the log house. He had to walk back to the house and Egbert helped

---
1 Unless otherwise noted, the source material for this chapter is from HFM or from the Hudgin family archive.

him hitch up a team of horses to pull the car out to the main road to Picton so he could get to the church on time.

A few weeks after they were married, the community came together to give Vernon and Mary a gift. It was presented to them with this letter:

Milford, January 4th, 1946

Dear Mary and Vernon,

You are no doubt aware that we are gathered here to-night to honour you on the occasion of your recent marriage.

We are very proud to be able to do this, as you, Vernon, are one of our South Marysburgh boys who answered the call to duty and service for King and Country. We are very thankful that you were spared to return to us after your experiences in active duty.

We believe that you have shown good judgment in the choice of a life partner. We wish you many years of happiness together.

You, Mary, are a stranger to many of us, but we trust that this will not be for long. We hope that you will enjoy yourself in this community and that you will find many congenial friends and neighbours.

We ask you to accept these gifts as a token of our good wishes.

Signed on behalf of your many friends,
Floral Minaker,
Janet Jeffrey,
Leila Hudgin,
Audrey Hicks.

Wedding day photo of Mary and Vernon (centre), 1945.
[Hudgin family archive.]

Chapter 6 — The Last Generations

After the wedding, Mary and Vernon stayed in Milford with Jennie and Egbert. In 1947, they moved into a house on Royal Street outside of town, and Vernon worked as a mechanic at Minaker's Garage in Milford (from 1945 to 1950). By 1946, their first child, Sherrie, was born, followed by their first son, Glen, in 1949. In 1950, they moved to Picton, into a house they rented on Mill Street (now known as Elk Street). Vernon had changed jobs and worked as a mechanic at both Sharpe Motors in Picton and McRae Motors closer to Waupoos. In 1952, he was unemployed for six weeks until he found a short stint working on the lake boats in the St. Lawrence River for approximately four months. As noted on an employment record that Vernon had filled out, he was employed by Colonial Ship Lines out of Port Colborne. When he returned to the County at the end of the shipping season that year, he took a position as a vehicle mechanic with the Royal Canadian Electrical and Mechanical Engineers (RCEME) in the Royal Canadian School of Artillery (Anti-Aircraft) at the airbase in Picton. No doubt Vernon's service in World War II helped him land this job. In addition to regular vehicle repairs and generator repairs, the vehicle mechanics, along with the radio mechanics, became involved in repairs to radio-controlled airplane targets. [2]

Vernon became a supervisor of the mechanics and was often involved with test-driving vehicles after repairs to ensure they were running properly. His son, Glen, remembers his dad driving the vehicles home, or to the log house (depending where they were staying at the time), and he recalls the excitement he felt when Vernon would come down the street in Jeeps, huge army trucks, fire trucks, ambulances and even amphibious vehicles. Sometimes Glen would get to sit in the vehicles and he remembers, as a small boy, having to climb up the large trucks to get in. Vernon may also have participated in some marine repair as the airbase had a 25-foot motor

---

2 Royal Canadian Electrical and Mechanical Engineers. *RCEME In The Royal Canadian School of Artillery (Anti-aircraft)*. 1955. p.3.

launch with a Chrysler marine engine which was used to recover target drogues and the radio controlled planes on the anti-aircraft range over Lake Ontario.[3]

By 1954, Mary was pregnant again and would share a story that she had a bad fall at the front of the house, down the steps, when she was expecting, but everything turned out well and she gave birth to another boy, Randy. The growing family needed more space so, in 1956, Vernon started building a house on Lake Street in Picton, with the help of his father, Egbert, who was, after all, a carpenter. (The house has since been torn down.) After the family moved to the Lake Street house, Mary had three more girls, Bonita (Bonnie), Wenda (Wendy) and Cinda (Cindy). The couple also became foster parents to many wards of the Children's Aid Society and adopted some of those children into their family, including Douglas Hudgin.

Vernon and Mary moved once again, this time to Maple Avenue in Picton, and they all continued to visit Egbert and Jennie out at the log house in the summers as the children grew up. The children have vivid memories of their time spent at the farm as it was foundational to their childhood. Even after Egbert and Jennie had moved to Picton, Vernon continued to visit and try to keep up the maintenance on the log home. When Egbert died in 1959, the property was passed to Vernon.[4] Apparently, Vernon paid his brother, Willard, for his share, and his sister, Mariam, agreed to the transfer.

Although Vernon and Mary lived in several houses in Picton and continued to use the log house as a summer home, gone were the days of farming the land, managing the hay or taking care of livestock. It was purely for recreational visits now. Throughout the summer, Vernon would drive back and forth to work in Picton and would return to the log house at

---

3 A drogue, in this case, was a target towed behind a boat or airplane. *Ibid.*
4 Land Registry Records, Prince Edward County Archives.

night. The kids had to wait until their dad got home before they were allowed to go swimming in Lake Ontario — sometimes a torturous wait on those hot summer days. The kids would sleep in the "front bedroom" upstairs, all in the same room, while Vernon and Mary would sleep in what they called the "back bedroom".

Glen and Wendy recall a large "puddle" the size of a small pond that was by the firebreak that separated the road from the military property. They and their siblings would use this as a swimming hole on hot days, especially since they were not allowed down to the lake without supervision! They have fond memories of walking the laneway to the lake and looking for rabbits and baby bunnies in the bushes.

One spring prior to 1967, the log house was burgled and many of the valuable items and antique furniture were stolen. Vernon had gone down to open up the house for the season and saw truck tire tracks leading up to the door of the east wing. He then discovered that the house had been broken into. Many of the family heirlooms were, unfortunately, lost. Mary loved collecting glassware and, over the years, had added pieces to a china cabinet that had been in the house for as long as anyone could remember. Many of these treasured items were taken as well.

By 1967, the kids were growing older, both Vernon and Mary were working and had a very busy household. They decided to sell the log house. There are differing stories on how Vernon came to this decision. One story is that Vernon, who was responsible for the debts from his parents' funerals, was being sued for the fees and, without any financial help from the family, had to sell the property. Another story is that Mary had her eye set on owning property in the Glenora area of the County from where her family originated and, since she dealt with most of the finances in the family, she made the call on selling the property. It was sold to Lillian Rose in 1967, for the sum of $7,000. Lillian paid Vernon half of that amount at the time of sale and Vernon agreed to hold a mortgage for the

Roses for the other $3,500. Regardless of the reason, we know that, years later, Vernon regretted the decision to sell and always talked about having the opportunity to buy back the property.

Even though the Hudgin family no longer owned the property, Vernon's children continued to visit the log house for nostalgic reasons; popping by on a Sunday drive, stopping to take a hike or have a picnic, often going down to the end of Ostrander Point Road for a dip in the lake. Glen remembers, as a teenager, driving down to the house in his 1962 Studebaker with his friend John Milner. They brought their sleeping bags and camped out at the neighbour's property in a little woodshed by the shoreline. The next day, they explored the shoreline and came across a boat with water in it, abandoned on the backside of the shore. They dragged it out to the beach and discovered there was a small hole in it, but they emptied the water out of the boat and put it into the lake. They jumped in and took a tin can with them to help bail any water from the small leak. They used washed-up wood boards as paddles and decided to paddle around the shoreline, bailing themselves out, jumping in and out of the boat, eventually deciding to let the waves drift them along, and they both fell asleep. They woke up to the boat filling with water, and Glen with a horrendous sunburn! Needless to say, his mother gave him "heck" as she treated him with vinegar and butter (a common treatment at the time), and told him never to get sunburnt again.

Glen and his siblings also started to bring their own children to the log house; sharing stories of yesteryears and family history, and reminiscing about their grandparents and their childhood. Fond memories include walking down to the lakeshore and combing the beach for wishing stones (rocks with holes through them), finding the best skipping rocks and looking for fossils.

They watched the log house decay as the decades passed. Bonnie and Glen made several attempts to buy the property back from the Roses, but

Chapter 6 — The Last Generations

to no avail. Mary passed away September 13, 2007 and Vernon passed away exactly 5 months later on February 13th, 2008. Vernon and Mary are buried at the Cherry Valley Cemetery in Prince Edward County.

Glen wrote a letter to the Roses shortly after his dad's death, again asking if they would be willing to sell; with no response:

> February 27, 2008
>
> Dear Mr. Rose
> We have spoken on the phone a couple of times in the past. You may recall that I was interested in having the first opportunity to purchase property that you own in South Marysburgh, if some day you decided to sell it. You and/or your wife had purchased the property from my father Vernon Hudgin about 1967. My great grandparents, grand parents and then my father had owned it. I remember it as a

Vernon's last visit to his great-grandfather's log house, c. 2000.
[Photo: Bonita (Hudgin) Allen.]

child as we would spend summers there. My Dad was born in that old log house. Dad talked about the old farm many times and I think he regretted ever selling it. I always kind of hoped that one day it would go up for sale and I might be able to acquire it and surprise Dad. Unfortunately Dad passed away two weeks ago so that will never happen now.

  In his memory I thought I would do a little research and put together a history record or scrapbook or something on the old farm. I recall Dad at times in the past making reference to Roses Lane and was wondering if that meant anything to you. Any history on the property or the surrounding area would really be appreciated, so I was hoping you would be kind enough to write back to me with any historical knowledge that you had.

  I have enclosed a self addressed stamped envelope for your convenience.

  Looking forward to any information you are able to share.

  Yours truly,

Glen Hudgin

Although the log house will never again belong to the Hudgin family, the family has put their faith and trust in the Nature Conservancy of Canada who purchased the land in 2018, and in the South Shore Joint Initiative, the local Prince Edward County community group who are now working to preserve and maintain the Moses Hudgin Log House and the history that it holds.

Chapter 7

Restoring the Moses Hudgin Log House

After the property was purchased by the Nature Conservancy of Canada in 2018 with the intent of protecting its biodiversity, the South Shore Joint Initiative (SSJI) took on the tenancy of the log house with the stated purpose of caring for and restoring it in collaboration with the Moses Hudgin Log House Restoration Committee. This committee was formed by members of SSJI, Hudgin family members, members of the Prince Edward Historical Society and other local people interested in preserving the historical and environmental landscapes of Prince Edward County. Through local fundraising campaigns, the committee intends to raise $150,000 towards restoration efforts which will return the log house to its original, circa 1860, appearance. The restoration will take a few years and will require the expertise of a heritage architect together with specialized contractors and builders who understand 19th Century construction methods.

Future efforts may include rebuilding the east wing, however, at the time this book is being written, the intent is to have the initial restoration look as original as possible to the 1860 time period. The goal is to make the interior a gathering space for field naturalists and for local events, as well as for possible use as a small museum to honour the Hudgin family and display some of the items that have been found during the clean-up and restoration. Electricity has now been installed for the first time ever on the property. This will help provide the opportunity for lighting, catering, and heat when the building is returned to practical functionality in 2023.

Many elements of the log house will need to be repaired in order to restore it, including the logs themselves, the chimney and the windows. The logs, while in remarkably good condition given their age, have weathered and the grain has opened up. This will require that the oils in the wood be replenished, which can be done by applying multiple coats of a double-boiled linseed oil formulation that will close the grain and extend the life of the logs.[1] Some of the logs will also need to be nudged back into alignment, as some have shifted outwards at the corners. This will be done by using a variety of methods such as temporary plates with canvas tie straps and ratchets or with threaded rods and nuts, depending on the resistance encountered. Once re-aligned, the logs can be reattached to each other with stainless steel threaded rods set into the logs and bonded with epoxy adhesive to strengthen the corners. Where the log structure has been weakened by later openings, the logs will be fastened to new infill framing in these openings for additional strength. A few logs have decayed and will most likely need replacing, as too will the lime-based chinking that helps seal the building. This will be replaced with a synthetic chinking with elastic characteristics, which is the modern equivalent to the original hot-lime mix. All of the floorboards will need replacing, as well as the staircase and, potentially, the floor of the

Open joints between logs, 2019
[From Edwin Rowse, "Moses Hudgin Log House Heritage Condition Assessment," 2019, p. 14.]

---

1   Edwin Rowse, "Moses Hudgin Log House Heritage Condition Assessment", 2019. p. 13.

second storey. This will be determined by an assessment of load capacity carried out by a registered structural engineer.²

The chimney on the east side of the house has deteriorated over time and will need rebuilding with new bricks to match the original details as closely as possible. Because the chimney is such a distinctive feature of the house and time period, it will be important to match its size, form and details, and also match the colour and texture of the bricks as far as possible.³

Historic photographs of the house show that the original windows deteriorated over time and were lost. Therefore, they will need replacing. The same photographs, along with site evidence indicate that they were originally 2-over-2 sliding sash windows, with the upper sashes having arched heads. This glazing pattern is different from the described attribute of 6-over-6 windows in the "Record of Designation" (see Heritage Designation By-Law, Appendix B). Following a presentation of detailed research to County Council's heritage advisory committee, this proposed revision to the window attribute has been recommended for approval. The window sash frames and panes will be fabricated to this revised 2-over-2 pattern. The original front door still exists; however, it will need extensive repairs to make it serviceable and airtight.⁴ The architect's drawings proposed for the restoration are included in Appendix E.

Surviving east chimney stack on the log house.
[From Edwin Rowse, "Moses Hudgin Log House Heritage Condition Assessment," 2019, p. 5.]

---

2 *Ibid*, pp. 13-17.
3 *Ibid.*, pp. 17-18.
4 *Ibid.*, p. 18.

Once these repairs and other exterior repairs and interior renovations are complete, it is hoped that future generations of not only the Hudgin family, but members of the general public, will be able to enjoy the Moses Hudgin Log House, to learn and appreciate the local history and the natural and built heritage of South Marysburgh and the South Shore of Prince Edward County.

Fifteen descendants of Moses Hudgin and Ann Mouck at the log house, 2020.
[Photo: Desirée Decoste, 2020]

L-R: The child in front is Veronica Mulder with her grandmother Sherrie (Hudgin) Davidson, Glen Hudgin, Terry Hudgin, Tracey (Hudgin) McBride, Laura (Hudgin) Edge, Matthew Edge, Julianna Edge, Bonita (Hudgin) Allen, Kelly Knott, Danielle Davidson, Christopher Hudgin with his children Logan and Anabel, Randy Hudgin.

---

4 Edwin Rowse, *ibid*. p. 18.

Chapter 7 — Restoring the Moses Hudgin Log House

Artist's concept drawing of the restored Moses Hudgin Log House, 2022.
[Sketch by Marjorie Cluett Seguin, 2022]

The Moses Hudgin Log House

Appendices

Appendix A – Hudgin/Rose Mortgage Document, 1967.

Appendix B – Heritage Designation Bylaw, 2011.

Appendix C – Mystery Document: Sale of Lot 4, from Charles Hudgin to Moses Hudgin (no date).

Appendix D – Deed of Land, from Sarah Ann Wilcox to Egbert Hudgin, 1922.

Appendix E – Architect's drawings proposed for the restoration, 2022.

Appendix A

Hudgin/Rose Mortgage Document, 1967

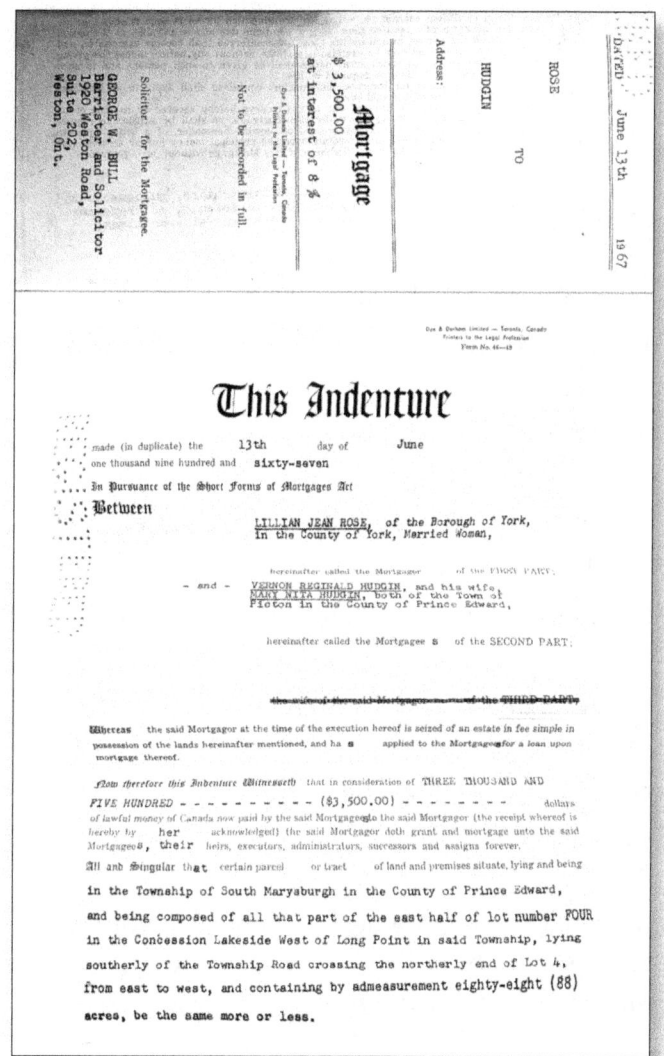

[Source: Hudgin family archive.]

Appendix B

Heritage Designation By-law, 2011

[County of Prince Edward Heritage Property Register, p. 165]

RECORD OF DESIGNATION: Moses Hudgins Log House

BY-LAW No. 2793-2011

Name of Municipality: Ward of South Marysburgh

Municipal Address of Property: Moses Hudgins Log House – 191 Ostrander Point Road

Owner of Property: N/A

Address of Owner: N/A

Date of Service of Notice of Intention to Designate: Ontario Heritage Trust & Owner - December 22, 2010

Dates of Publication of Notice of Intention: The County Weekly News – Dec 23, 2010

Dates of Publication of Notice of Passing of By-law: The County Weekly News – Feb 14, 2011

Date of Designating By-law: February 8, 2011

Reason for Designation:

Design Value
It is of unusually late (c. 1865) log design comprising one and a half stories. It therefore remains a rarity in Prince Edward County, especially considering frame construction was common by this date. Built in an area where

cedar trees were cut for shingles, the square logs are cedar, an unusual material for log houses. The lap joints are hewn to 5" rather than the typical 8". The chimney design is consistent to a pre-1870 design. The steep roof is a County feature.

Contextual Value:
Belden's Atlas (1878) shows the log house on its original 100 acres which ended at the lake allowing Moses to fish and sail as well as farm. These were the usual economic realities of the day for an area of unfertile land. The house still sits in its original location close to and facing Ostrander Point Road.

Cultural Heritage Attributes:
Original location facing Ostrander Point Road
Size & form
Unusually late cedar log construction
Unusual five-inch lap joints
Chimney of County form prior to 1870
Steep-pitched roof, a County form
~~6-over-6 windows~~ (under review, 2021)

Property Description:
The subject lands are described as Part of Lot 4, Concession West of Long Point, civic address 191 Ostrander Point Road, Ward of South Marysburgh, in the Municipality of the County of Prince Edward.

Date: April 28, 2011

[Source: Prince Edward County Record of Designation. Retrieved July 2022: https://www.thecounty.ca/wp-content/uploads/2020/08/PEC-Record-of-Designation-with-Pics-public-version-Nov-2019.pdf]

Appendix C

Mystery Document

Sale of Lot 4 from Charles Hudgin(s) to Moses Hudgin(s) (no date)

[Source: Hudgin family archive.]

Know all men by these presents, that I Charles Hudgins of the Township of Marysburgh in the County of Prince Edward and Province of Canada, Yeoman, of and in consideration of the sum of Five Hundred dollars lawful money of the said Province to me in hand paid by Moses Hudgins of Long Point in the Township and County aforesaid, Yeoman, the receipt whereof is hereby acknowledged have bargained, sold, assigned and quitted claim and by these presents do bargain, sell, assign and Quit Claim to the said Moses Hudgins, his Heirs and assigns for ever all my right title, interest estate property claim and demand both at Law and in Equity and as well in expectancy as is in possession to all and singular that tract or parcel of Land situate in the Township of Marysburgh, County and Province aforesaid containing by admeasurement One Hundred acres be the same more or less being composed of the East half of Lot Number four on Long Point to have and to Hold the above assigned premises with all the privileges and appurtenances there of to Him the said Moses Hudgins his heirs and assigns to their own use forever

over

Appendix D

Deed of Land
From Sarah Ann Wilcox to Egbert Hudgin, 1922

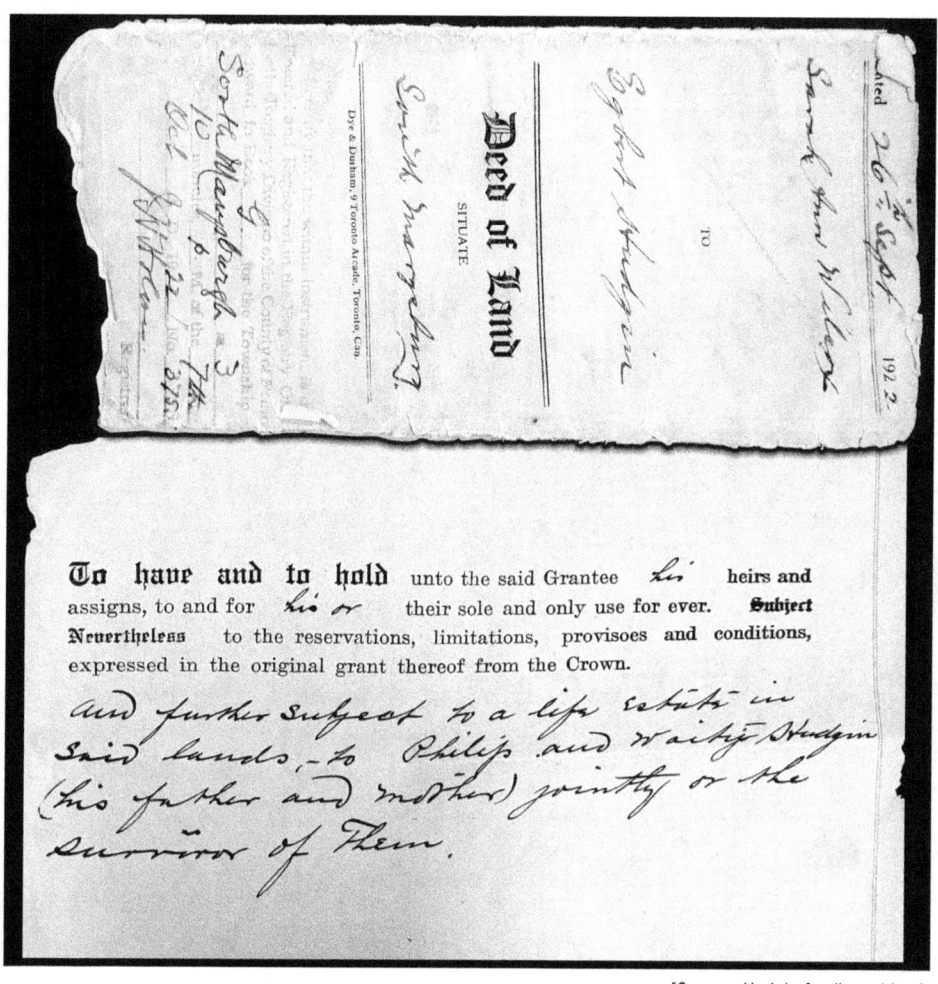

[Source: Hudgin family archive.]

Appendix E

Architect's drawings proposed for the Restoration of the Moses Hudgin Log House, 2022

These drawings are the property of Edwin Rowse Architecture Inc. and may not be used or reproduced without expressed approval. Refer to engineering drawings before proceeding with work. The contractor shall verify all dimensions and levels on site and report any discrepancies to the Architect before beginning work. Do not scale from the drawings. Use figured dimensions only. The contactor is responsible for any changes made to the drawings without the architect's approval.

EDWIN ROWSE
Architecture Inc.

PROJECT

MOSES HUDGIN LOG HOUSE RESTORATION, PHASE 3 EXTERIOR ENVELOPE

ADDRESS   191 OSTRANDER POINT RD, SOUTH MARYSBURGH

[Courtesy of Edwin Rowse.]

SITE NORTH

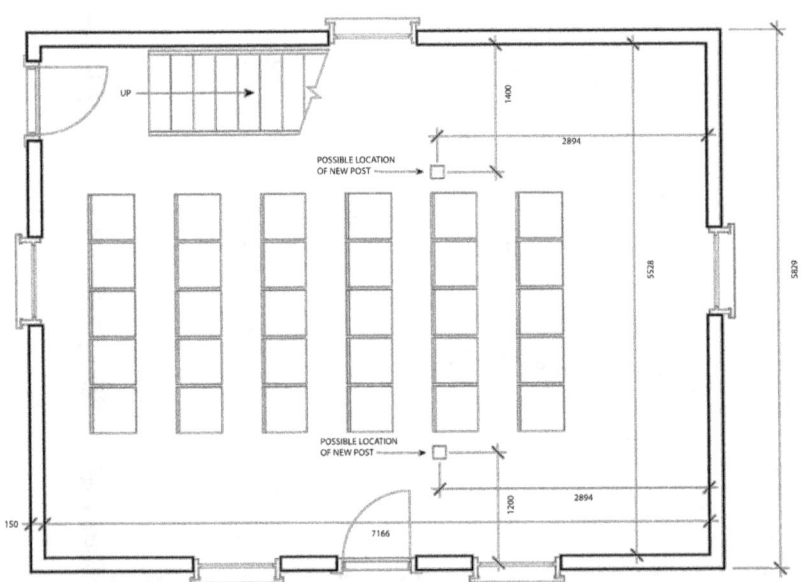

GROUND FLOOR PLAN
AF-1

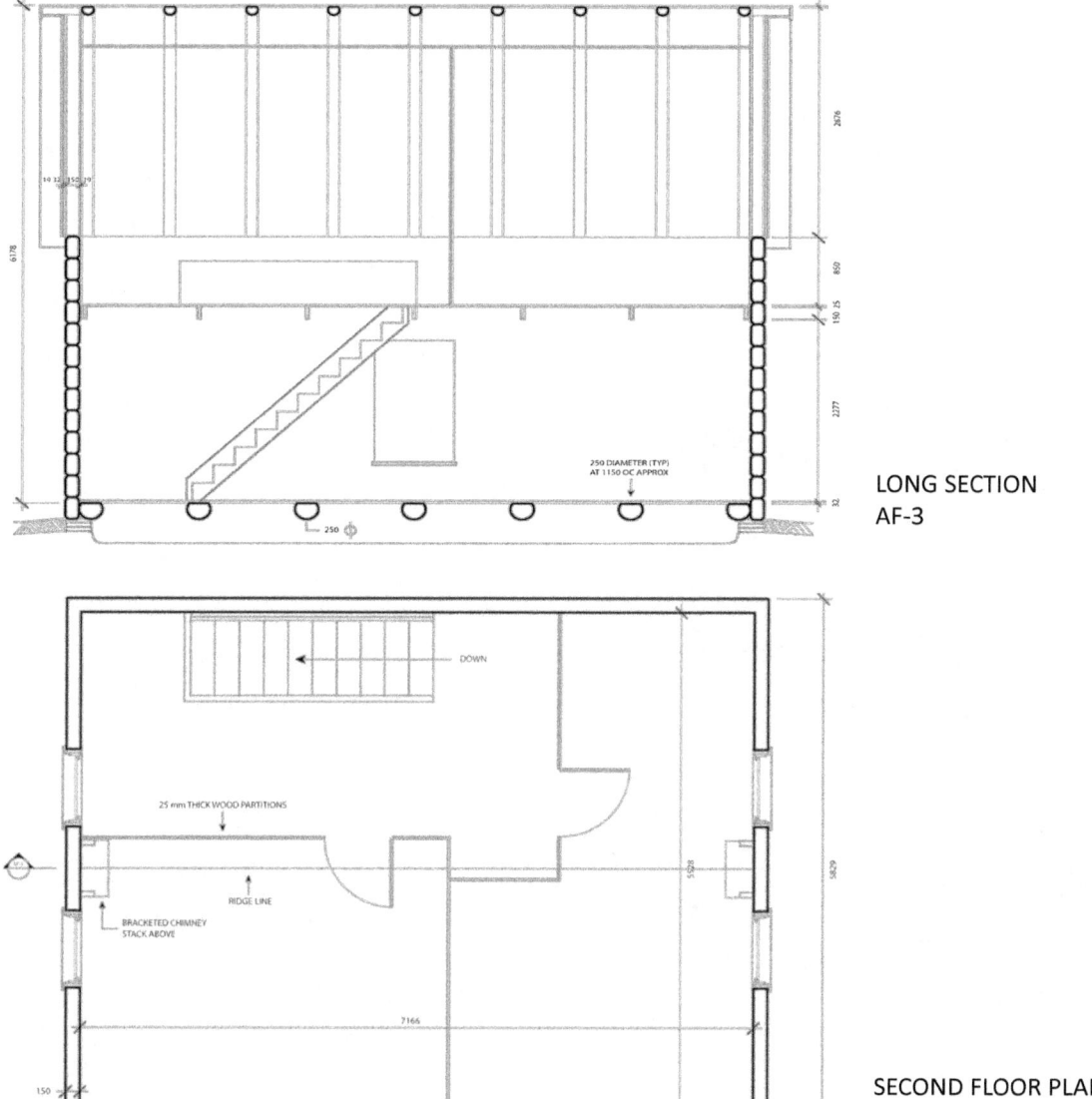

LONG SECTION
AF-3

SECOND FLOOR PLAN
AF-2

The Moses Hudgin Log House

Sources Cited

Ackerman, Gerald, with Historical Committee (Howard Dulmage, Quentin Minaker, Myrtle Robbins, Maurice Clapp). *History of South Bay United Church.*

Ackerman, Gerald. *The History of Cheesemaking in Prince Edward County.* Milford, 2001.

Archives Ontario. "Finding Land Registry Documents, 2020." Retrieved July, 2022: http://www.archives.gov.on.ca/en/access/documents/research_guide_231_finding_land_registration_records.pdf.

Archives Ontario. MS 658 reel 287, Marysburgh Ts., Folio 1241/44: Grant to Michael Mouck, Marysburgh, 100 acres, 29 Oct 1802.

Belden, H. & Co., *Illustrated Historical Atlas of the Counties of Hastings and Prince Edward*, Toronto, 1878.

Belleville Intelligencer, February 3, 1881.

Campbell, Steve. *Light Houses of Prince Edward County*, Bloomfield, 2016.

Canada. Department of National Defence. "Practicing UXO safety in Prince Edward County, Ontario, 2017." Retrieved July, 2022: https://www.canada.ca/en/department-national-defence/services/uxo/uxo-locations/practicing-uxo-safety-prince-edward-county.html.

Canniff, William. *History of the Settlement of Upper Canada.* Toronto, 1869.

Catling, P.M., and S.M. McKay-Kuja, B. Kostiuk, and A. Kuja. "Ostrander Point Vascular Plants, 2014." Retrieved July, 2022: https://peptbo.ca/photos/custom/PDFs/Ostrander%20Point%20Vascular%20Plants%20-%208-26.pdf.

Census of Canada. 1871, 1881, 1891, 1901, 1911, 1921.

Census of Canada West. 1861.

Cole, Dr. Paul. "Hudgin Genealogy." Kingston, Ontario, Canada.

Cruickshank, Tom & Peter John Stokes. *The Settler's Dream.* Picton, 1984.

Dulmage, Howard. *Memories of South Bay.* Picton, 1980.

Fairfield, Dora. *Dora's Cookbook.* Hunter, Rose & Co., 1888.

Library and Archives Canada. "Disbanded Men from the German Troops Settled in Township No. 5, Bay of Quinte, October 4th, 1784." Series B, Volume 168.

Metcalfe, Willis. *Canvas and Steam on Quinte Waters*. South Bay, 1979.

Metcalfe, Willis. *Memories of Yesteryears*. Picton, 1977.

Metcalfe, Willis, "Scrapbooks". Prince Edward County Archives.

Mika, Nick & Helma. *The Settlement of Prince Edward County*. Belleville, 1984.

Montagnes, James. "Mail in Miniature." *MacLean's Magazine*. September 15, 1943. Retrieved July 2022: https://archive.macleans.ca/article/1943/9/15/mail-in-miniature

Montreal Weekly Witness. June 13, 1888.

National Board of Lake Underwriters. *Valuation In Currency on a Cash Basis*. Buffalo, N.Y., 1874. Retrieved July, 2022: https://images.maritimehistoryofthegreatlakes.ca/122849/page/86?q=olivia&docid=MHGL.122849.

North Marysburgh Museum Board. "Marysburgh Settlement. First Records, Council 1850."

Pasternak, Suzanne. *The Vanishing Legacy: The History of the Lake Faring Families in Prince Edward County. South Bay, Ontario.* Videorecording – DVD, 2014.

Picton Gazette. Death Announcement. March 7th, 1952.

Prince Edward County Archives. "Heritage Architectural Survey of Prince Edward" (HASPE) files.

Prince Edward County Archives. Land Registry Records.

Prince Edward County. Record of Designation. Retrieved July 2022: https://www.thecounty.ca/wp-content/uploads/2020/08/PEC-Record-of-Designation-with-Pics-public-version-Nov-2019.pdf]

Prince Edward Heritage Advisory Committee. "Barker and Wilson, the Iron Men of Picton." *Heritage Walking Tour of Picton* brochure. Retrieved July, 2022: https://www.peclibrary.org/wp-content/uploads/2020/04/Heritage_Committee_BarkerandWilsonTheIronMenofPicton_walking_path.pdf.

Proctor, Charles. *200 Years of Hudgins*. Toronto, 1976.

Prinyer, John. *Looking Backward: Some Early History and Progress of the Township of Marysburgh*. Picton, 1890.

Rainey, Daniel and Helen Tompkins. *The Educational Tapestry of Athol, North and South Marysburgh Townships Prince Edward County 1800-1966*. Belleville, 2015.

Sources Cited

Rowse, Edwin. "Moses Hudgin Log House Heritage Condition Assessment." South Shore Joint Initiative, 2019.

Royal Canadian Electrical and Mechanical Engineers. "RCEME In The Royal Canadian School of Artillery (Anti-aircraft)." 1955. Retrieved July, 2022: https://archive.org/details/rceme-in-the-royal-canadian-school-of-artillery-antiaircraft/page/n3/mode/2up.

Sawchuk, Larry and Burke, Stacie. "Mortality in an Early Ontario Community: Belleville 1876-1885," *Urban History Review*, Vol. 29. No. 1. October, 2000.

Shanahan, David. "Land for Goods: The Crawford Purchase." *Anishinabek News.* November 8, 2018. Retrieved July, 2022: http://anishinabeknews.ca/2018/11/08/land-for-goods-the-crawford-purchases/

Simcoe, J.G. *Simcoe's Military Journal.* New York, 1844.

Seguin, Marc. *For Want of a Lighthouse: Guiding Ships Through the Graveyard of Lake Ontario, 1828-1914.* Prince Edward County, 2019.

South Shore Joint Initiative. "Historic Log House Restoration, 2020." Retrieved July, 2022: https://www.ssji.ca/historic_log_house_restoration.

South Shore Joint Initiative. "Proposal for Conservation Reserve designation for Ostrander Point Crown Land Block and Point Petre Provincial Wildlife Area." Retrieved July, 2022: https://www.ssji.ca/ conservation_reserve_proposal_for_south_shore.

Snider, C.H.J. "Schooner Days". *Toronto Telegram.* August 17th, 1946

Spafford, P.K. *As I Remember Prince Edward County and Beyond.* Picton, 1998.

Tremaine, George C. *Tremaine's Map of the County of Prince Edward Upper Canada.*, Toronto, 1863.

United Empire Loyalist Centennial Committee. *The Centennial of the Settlement of Upper Canada by the United Empire Loyalists, 1784-1884,* Toronto, 1885.

U.S. Department of Commerce and Labor, Bureau of the Census. *Heads of Families at the First Census of the United States Taken in the Year 1790 – Virginia.* Washington, 1908.

"Whose Land." Retrieved July, 2022: https://www.whose.land/en/treaty/ crawford-purchase-1783.

Wilson, Alan. *The Clergy Lands of Upper Canada.* The Canadian Historical Association Booklet No. 23. Ottawa, 1969.

THE MOSES HUDGIN LOG HOUSE

INDEX

—A—
Adolphustown, 19
Airgraph, 60
Algiers Algeria, 61
American Revolution, 17, 18, 19
Anishinaabeg, 17
Anti-Aircraft range, 76
Anti-Aircraft School, See Royal Canadian School of Artillery (Anti-Aircraft)
Ashley, William, 46
Athol Township, 40
Austin, Willet, 46

—B—
Babcock, Rev. R. 51
Babylon Road, 28, 39, 58
Babylon School, 28, 48, 49, 58
Barley Days, 35, 44
Bay of Quinte, 17, 18, 21, 33, 73
Bedbourgh, Keith, 63
Belden Atlas, 1878, 14, *7n*, 15, 91
Belleville, 37
Benson's canning factory, 64
Black Creek, 35
Blanche schooner, 42
Bongard, Amy Helena, 25
　George Washington, 25, *25n*, 45
　J.J., 46

Bongard, Lulu, 25
　Mary Louise, 25
　Waity L., wife of Philip Hudgin, 24, *25n*, 41, 51, 52, *52n*
Borden, Camp, 59
Bosko, Rev. N., 51
Brown, Esther, wife of William Hudgin Sr., 19

—C—
Cannon, Abraham, 46
Case, Harmon, 12
Cherry Valley, 23, 64, 79
Chicago, 22
Claus (or Klus), Susannah, 21
Collier family, 39, 41
Collier, Margaret, 64, *64n*
Collier, Nancy Ann, Ann Mouck's mother, 20, 22
Collins, John, surveyor, 17
Colonial Ship Lines, 75
Consumption, 36, 37
Cook, George, 56
Cornwall Ontario, 59
Cornwallis. General, Lord, 19
Crawford Purchase, 18
Crawford William Redford, 18

—D—
Darvel Scotland, 60
Davidson, Danielle, 84

Index

Deed, Lot 4, Sarah to Egbert, 50, Appendix D
Department of National Defence (DND), 58, 70
Duke of Argyll, troopship, 60
Dulmage, Howard, 44

—E—
east wing of the log house, 8, 10, 11, 41 42, 43, 77, 81
Edge, Julianna, 84
    Matthew, 84
    Ryan, *5n*
Elk Street, 75
England, 60, 61

—F—
F.F. Cole, schooner, 46
Fairfield, Dora, 32
False Ducks Island, 45
Farrington, George, 31
Fifth Town, 7, see also Marysburgh
fishing, 17, 24, 25, 34, 44, 46, 47, 55, 91

—G—
Gamball, Dr. Robert, 37
Gananoque, 18
Genier, Mary Eliza/Marylise, wife of Lewis Hudgin, 24, 33
German soldiers, 20, 21
Germany, 21
Glenora, 73, 77
Gloucester County, Virginia, 18
Greenock Scotland, 59
Gunshot Treaty, 18

—H—
Haldimand, Sir Frederick, 18

Halifax, Nova Scotia, 59, 61
Hallowell Township, 40
Hanna, Keith, 43, 47, 52, 69
Hastings and Prince Edward Regiment (Hasty P's), 60
Haudenosaunee, 18
Heritage Advisory Committee, 7, 83, Appendix B
Hicks, Audrey, 74
    Gena, 24
    J. Miller, 23
    Jacob, 45, 46
    Michael, 23
    Olivia, 36
    William Ira, 23
Hineman, Welden W., 50
Hudgin, Amelia Ann (Hughes), 40, 41, 44, 48, 50
    Amy Therese (McConnell), 25, 39
    Anabel, 84
    Andrew, 22, *22n*
    Bonita/Bonnie (Allen), 1, 2, *61n*, 71, 73, 76, 78
    Carol, 64
    Charles, brother of Moses Hudgin, 14, Appendix C
    Charles, son of Michael Hudgin, 23, 39, 46
    Charlotte (Hicks), 23
    Christopher, 84
    Cinda/Cindy (Benson), 76
    Douglas, 76
    Egbert, 9, 12, *28n*, 40, 41, 47-51, 54-58, 63, 65-71, 73, 75, 76, Appendix D
    Eliza Jane (Bongard), 25, *25n*, 39
    Eric, 64, 66, 70
    Eunice, 64
    Floyd, 63, 70
    Glendon/Glen, 1, 2, 12, 57, 59, 66, 68, 69, 75, 77, 78, 79, 80, 84
    Laura Lee (Hineman), 41
    Laura L. (Edge), 84

Hudgin, Lewis, cousin of Moses Hudgin, 45
    Lewis, great-grandfather of Moses Hudgin, 3
    Lewis, son of Moses Hudgin, 24, 28
    Logan, 84
    Mariam (Molyneux) (Vance), 50, 55, 64, 65, 71, 76
    Michael, 23, 28, 29, 40
    Mildred E. (Bigg), 41, 51
    Philip, 10, 24, 28, 39-52
    Randy, 76, 84
    Ronda, 64
    Sarah Ann (Rorke) (Wilcox) 22, 39, 40, 41, 55, Appendix D
    Sherrie (Davidson), 52, 71, 75, 84
    Solomon, 24, 28, 36, 37, 41
    Terry, 64, 66, 67, 68, 70, 71, 84
    Tracey (McBride), 84
    Vernon, 1, 2, 9, 50-52, 55, 57, 59-65, 70, 73-79
    Wait, 24, 28, 39
    Wenda/Wendy (Kennedy), 46, 68, 69, 77
    Willard, 9, 55, 62, 63, 64, 69, 76
    William Jr., 19, 20
    William Sr., 18, 19, 20
    see also Family Tree, 5
Hudgin tenant house, 16, 23, 24
Hudgin-Rose Nature Reserve, 2
Hughes, Edna, 52
    George R., 50
    Mary Esther, wife of Michael Hudgin, 23, 33

—I—
Indigenous peoples, 17
Inveraray Scotland, 60
Ireland, 20, 73

—J—
Jackson's Falls school, 49
Jeffrey, Janet, 74

—K—
King George III, 17
Kingston, 59, 61
Knott, Kelly, 84

—L—
Lake Ontario, 12, 14, 21, 34, 35, 42, 44, 45, 46, 47, 76, 77
Lake Street, 76
Lennox County, Incorporated Militia, 19
life expectancy, 36, *36n*
life saving station, 25, 45
lifeboat crew, 45, 46
Long Point harbour, 45, 46
Long Point, 12, 23, 45, 46, 92
Loyalists, 17, 18, 19

—M—
Maple Avenue, 76
Marr, Esther, second wife of William Hudgin Jr., 20
Marysburgh, 7, 9, 12, 13, 15, *16n*, 17, 18, 19, 20, 21, *21n*, 22, 27, *28n*, *31n*, 34, 35, 37, 40, *40n*, 51, 52, *52n*, 54, 55, 57, 65, 74, 79, 84, 90
Mathews County, Virgina, 18
McConnell, Ella Ann, *64n*
    George, 55
    Henry, 25, *55n*
    Jennie, wife of Egbert Hudgin, 50, 54-57, 60, *61n*, 62-66, 71, 75, 76
    Mrs. Henry, 51
    Percy L., 25

Index

McRae Motors, 75
Methodist Church, 13, 29, 30, 37, 49, 57
Milford Circuit, 29, 30
Milford, 13, 22, 25, 30, 35, 43, 54, 55, 56, 71, 74, 75
militia, 19
Mill Street, 75
Minaker, Floral, 74
    Lyall, 63
Minaker's Garage, 75
Mississaugas, 17
Molyneaux, Gary, 65
Molyneaux, Neil, 65
    Wallace, 65
Montreal, 21
Mouck, Ann, wife of Moses Hudgin 1, 12, 20, 21, 51, 84
Mouck, Capt. Ryan, 23
    Gottlieb, 21, *21n*
    Leyda, 50
    Michael, father of Ann Mouck, 12, *22n*
    Walter, 25
    William, 22
Mulder, Veronica, 84

—N—

Nature Conservancy of Canada (NCC), 1, 80, 81
New Brunswick, 18, 19
New Connexion Methodists, 29
North Marysburgh, see Marysburgh

—O—

O'Neil, Mary N., wife of Vernon Hudgin, 73-79
Olivia, schooner, 36
Onagara River, 18
Ontario Heritage Act, 7, Appendix B
Ostrander Point Road, 1, *15n*, 16, 50, 58, 78, 90, 91
Oswego New York, 35

—P—

Palmatier, Daniel, 45
    Ephraim, 46
Petawawa, 63
Philadelphia, 19
Picton, schooner, 24, 25
Picton, town, 25, 30, 32, 33, 39, 46, 51, 56. 62, 64, 65, 71, 75, 76
Point Traverse, 12, 20, 24, 25, 44, 45, *45n*, 46, 51
Poplar Point lifesaving station, 25, 44, 45, *45n*
Port Milford, 13, 36, 44, 57
Pounder, Roland, 70
Preston, Henry, 46
Prince Edward Point lighthouse, see Point Traverse
Prinyer, John, 34
Prinyer's Cove, 34
Proctor, Charles, 16, 23, 47

—Q—

Queen's Rangers, 19
Quinte, Bay of, see Bay of Quinte

—R—

Red Onion, 45, see also Point Traverse
Regent Theatre, 56, *56n*, 64
RMS Andes, troopship, 59
Rorke, Edward S., 22, 40
    James, 22, 39
    Sarah E., 40
Rose, Ben, 79
    John, 20
    Lillian, 1, *77*, 78, Appendix A
Rowse, Edwin, 11, 82, 83, Appendix E
Royal Street, Milford, 25, 55, 75
Royal Canadian Electrical and Mechanical Engineers (RCEME), 75

Index

Royal Canadian School of Artillery (Anti-Aircraft), 75
Royal Crescent Cheese Factory, 55

–S–

Salmon Point, 45, *45n*
schooling, 28, *28n*, 29, 48, 49, 57, 58
Scotland, 59, 60
Sharpe Motors, 75
Sicily, 60, *61n*
Simcoe, John Graves, 19
Smith E.H., 58
South Bay Church, 13, 29, 30, 49, 57
South Bay Point lighthouse, 45, see also Point Traverse
South Bay, 22, 35, 44, 46, 50, 51, 52, 62
South Shore Joint Initiative, 2, 80, 81
South Marysburgh, see Marysburgh
Spafford, Kitty, wife of Wait Hudgin, 24
    Leroy, father of Kitty Spafford, 45, 46
    Marshall, 45
St. Lawrence River, 75
Staffordshire figurine, 69

–T–

Toniata River, 18
Toronto, 19, 51
Tremaine Map, 1863, 7, 13, 14
Trenton, 24
Tuberculosis, see Consumption

–U–

United Church, see Methodist Church
United Empire Loyalists, see Loyalists
United States, 35, 43
Unterellen, Germany, 21
Upper Canada, 18, 19, *20n*

–V–

Vance, Wilson, 65
Vandusen, Jacob, 12
Virginia, 3, 18, 19
Vorce, Marcellus, 46

–W–

Walters, Rex, 63
War of 1812, 19, 20
Wattham, Henry, 41
Wesleyan Methodists, 29, 30
Wilcox, Oliver, 23, 41
Wilson, Charles S., 14, 39
Wood, David, 45, 46
Woodrous Corners, 41
World War II, 59, 73, 75
Wright, Rachel, first wife of William Hudgin, Jr., mother of Moses Hudgin, 20

–Y–

York County, New Brunswick, 19
York, Upper Canada, 19
Yorktown, Virginia, battle, 19

www.ingramcontent.com/pod-product-compliance
Lightning Source LLC
Chambersburg PA
CBHW060500010526
44118CB00018B/2484